P9-EAN-900

DATE DUE

JE 22 95			
FE 1 0 00			
DE 17 03			
MY 31 05			

WALL STREET WOMEN

WALL STREET WOMEN

Anne B. Fisher

Alfred A. Knopf

New York   1990

This Is a Borzoi Book Published by Alfred A. Knopf, Inc.

Copyright © 1989 by Anne B. Fisher
All rights reserved under International and Pan-American Copyright
Conventions. Published in the United States by Alfred A. Knopf, Inc.,
New York, and simultaneously in Canada by Random House of
Canada Limited, Toronto. Distributed by Random House, Inc.,
New York.

Library of Congress Cataloging-in-Publication Data
Fisher, Anne B., [date]
Wall Street women / Anne B. Fisher.—1st ed.
p. cm.
Includes index.
ISBN 0-394-55271-7
1. Women in finance—New York (N.Y.)   2. Wall Street.   I. Title.
HD6073F472U64   1990
332.6'088042—dc20   89-45310   CIP

Manufactured in the United States of America
First Edition

For my parents, Philip and Julie,
and for Michael, my own white knight.

When I got to Donaldson, Lufkin & Jenrette in the late sixties, the women they were hiring were either socialite debutantes or had really big boobs. I was the only "girl" there who was serious about a career. So I left. *—A female securities analyst and portfolio manager, now earning over $1 million a year at another firm*

There is no business so neurotic, fanciful, scared of its own shadow and downright loony as the money business. *—Robertson Davies*

People think Wall Street is terribly glamorous, and sometimes it is. But it's also falling asleep in the L.A. airport in the same clothes you've been wearing for three days. Trying to change a $100 bill in the cab line at La Guardia. Sitting at your desk sending out for pizza at 5 a.m. when you've been working all night.
—A female investment banker who specializes in mergers and acquisitions

Money, which represents the prose of life . . . is, in its effects and laws, as beautiful as roses. *—Ralph Waldo Emerson*

ACKNOWLEDGMENTS

I'm grateful to the hundreds of people who helped in the reporting for this book, especially to the scores of women and men on Wall Street who were patient in their explanations, candid in their opinions, and generous with their time. Thanks are due also to the public-relations people at Salomon Brothers, Merrill Lynch, and Chase Manhattan, for letting me wander around loose in their trading rooms, which are usually off limits to reporters; and to the editors of *Fortune* magazine, whose forbearance and encouragement have allowed me to labor through several drafts of this book without feeling that I have burned any bridges behind me.

If not for Freya Manston's ingenuity, Corona Machemer's wisdom, and Barbara Loos's friendship, it's highly unlikely that I'd have written this book at all. To them, a thousand hugs and roses.

CONTENTS

I.
THE WORLD THEY
WORK IN

On October 19, 1987, as the spectacular five-year bull market skidded to a shuddering halt, Elaine Garzarelli was one of the few professionals on Wall Street with little cause for panic or despair, or even regret. An executive vice president and the chief quantitative market analyst at Shearson Lehman Hutton, she had devised a computerized statistical method for predicting the stock market's direction. As one of her clients told *Institutional Investor* magazine, "Elaine's method is different from any other on Wall Street. For one thing, it *works*."

And it did. On October 12, a full week ahead of the Crash, Elaine told viewers of Cable News Network's *MoneyLines* that it was already past time to get out of stocks. Her own clients, mostly huge institutions such as banks and insurance companies with billions at stake, had taken her word for it over the preceding six weeks and were well out of the storm, sitting on piles of cash and bonds. Black Monday found Elaine at her desk in her vast office with its wide, silvery view of the East River, eyeing her Quotron screen with comparative calm. Even as the Dow plunged a harrowing 500 points in the last two hours of trading, shares of the Sector Analysis Portfolio—a mutual fund, with $700 million in assets, which Elaine had started in August and still manages—defied gravity, *up* 59 cents by the closing bell.

Uptown, at PaineWebber's art-studded mid-Manhattan head-quarters, no such serenity prevailed. Joyce Fensterstock, a managing director in charge of Mitchell Hutchins Asset Management's mutual fund business and a board member of several other PaineWebber subsidiaries, spent the morning of October 19 being pulled into and out of a routine meeting of the board of directors of PaineWebber Development Corp. "My money managers were all in shock. It was like *'This is not real,'*" she said later. "*'This can't be happening.'*"

Joyce and her staff reacted quickly, selling hundreds of thousands of shares on the morning of October 20, when prices briefly rebounded, so that Mitchell Hutchins's mutual funds raked in more than enough cash to cover the claims of investors who pulled out of the market during the gloomy weeks that followed. In the meantime, Joyce had put in a long night of frantic telephone calls. One crash-induced crisis was the closing of the stock exchange in Hong Kong, where Mitchell Hutchins, like most sophisticated mutual funds, had invested heavily in the giddy days of ever-soaring prices. With Hong Kong shut down, and no prices available, investors in American funds were left in the dark as to what their shares were worth, and hence doubly inclined to panic. "Everyone was desperate for information. It felt like the end of the world," Joyce said afterward. "And over the following couple of weeks—this is my personal barometer of stress—every single person at PaineWebber got sick. Colds, flu, viruses. *Everybody.*"

On the evening of October 19, 1987, several hundred Merrill Lynch brokers gathered at the American Museum of Natural History. The occasion was a bash, planned months in advance, to fête the success of the firm's star producers, those who generated the fattest commissions for themselves and the firm. Having watched in horror as the market plummeted, all the while fielding phone calls from terrified clients and trying with maddening lack of success to sell, sell, sell as the swamped stock exchanges slowed to a bewildered crawl, the beaten brokers nevertheless donned their black ties, sequins, satin, and spangles and trooped off to their gala evening.

Judy Connolly, one of Merrill's top brokers for more than a decade, was among them. Most of her clients' wealth having been tucked away in government bonds over the preceding months, Judy was relatively unrattled. Still, October 19 was, she recalls, "awful. On my way to the party I stopped off at my boyfriend's office. He's a doctor. I wanted to lie down for a while in one of his consulting rooms. So I'm lying there, and I'm waiting for somebody to come and put a lily in my hands. Then we get to the room Merrill had rented for the evening, at the museum, and it turns out to be the oceanography section. So you come down this long Art Deco staircase, and the band is playing, and you look up at the belly of an enormous whale." She laughs. "It was perfect! It was just like being on the *Titanic!*" Determined to have a good time, the brokers, pale and shaken, lined up at the bar, ordered double scotches, and talked about everything but work. "There was a sense that this might be the last party for a long time to come," Judy observes. "So we were all thinking, 'Well, eat, drink, and be merry, for tomorrow we die.'"

The revelers had a point. Amid a wave of Wall Street layoffs and cutbacks over the next months, Merrill Lynch made known that some two thousand employees might be dismissed, and brokers who remained would see their pay sliced by a total of $200 million. That, at least, was only money. At E. F. Hutton, where brokers braced for sudden unemployment as their firm merged with Shearson Lehman Brothers, some worried for their lives, and with good reason. In late October, a furious investor walked into a Merrill Lynch office in Miami and shot his broker and another employee. The broker died. Brenda Landry, a securities analyst at Morgan Stanley, is married to an E. F. Hutton broker whose frenetic phone calls after the Crash included a death threat from a client. "It's hard enough watching so many of your friends losing their jobs, and seeing your own wealth shrinking because your stocks have gone through the floor, and knowing that your year-end bonus is going to be lousy," said Brenda. "But *death:* that's one thing we never expected to worry about."

The shocks of overnight austerity, not surprisingly, struck most bitterly at those who had never seen lean times on the Street before, and had thus managed to persuade themselves that the bull market that had begun in 1982 would go on forever. From her perspective as a twenty-year veteran of the market's gyrations, Kristin Gamble, for one, knew better. A money manager and partner in the investment firm Flood, Gamble Associates, Kristin started her career as an analyst at Merrill Lynch in 1968. She remembers only too vividly what happened in 1974, an "absolutely devastating" year, in which many stocks—including some of the much-vaunted Nifty 50—lost 80 percent of their value. "The market fell relentlessly, month after month. You used to come into the office every day praying that the phone wouldn't ring, because you didn't want to talk to clients," she says.

In many ways, the five-year runup in stock prices that ended in the fall of 1987 was nothing new—just the latest, longest, and loudest variation on a very old theme. "On the way up, you always hear all kinds of 'new era' arguments, claiming that what goes up isn't coming down. In the eighties the idea was that Japanese stocks were trading at price-earnings ratios twice as high as ours, so the sky was supposed to be the limit," she noted. "But I've never heard a 'new era' argument that turned out to be accurate. And this time everything got exaggerated because you had a whole new crop of people on the Street, and a whole new flood of first-time investors, who had never seen a bear market and just couldn't imagine it."

In some respects, however, the bull market did create a new era on Wall Street, opening up unheard-of opportunities for a long-neglected pool of talent: women. The year 1987 was a milestone.

In January, as the Dow Jones Industrial Average topped off a hyperactive twelve months by barreling past the 2,000 mark for the first time ever, four of the Street's most august investment banks could point to less conspicuous firsts of their own: two new partners and four freshly appointed managing directors (the equivalent of partnership in publicly held firms) who happened to be female. Of the scores of top-level promotions Wall Street securities houses handed out, six may seem a tiny number, and of course it is. But it nearly doubled, in one fell swoop, the total number of Wall Street women in positions of real power — not to mention with annual compensation in the seven-figure stratosphere. "The big investment banks have been a little slow off the mark in rewarding women," conceded a male partner at one firm, in what many Wall Streeters would regard as an egregious understatement. "But women are beginning to come into their own now, and you'll see many more reaching the top in the next few years."

He was very likely right. As the turbulent eighties subsided, the roll call was still short, but growing steadily longer. Lazard Frères, an elegant little investment bank that has been around more than 140 years, finally named its first woman partner, Marilyn LaMarche. Morgan Stanley & Co., meanwhile, is often perceived by outsiders as one of the stuffiest and most hidebound of the prestigious old-line investment banks. Yet in 1986 the firm boasted eight female principals, the level of management just below managing director, and three of them — Karen Bechtel, Catherine James, and Marie-Elaine A. LaRoche — moved up to managing directorships in 1987, followed by three more women a year later.

Salomon Brothers, the giant trading powerhouse, lagged a little, appointing only one female managing director, Barbara Alexander, as of January 1987. But "Solly," as Wall Streeters call it, also named a half dozen women directors — a new title above vice president, created just the year before, that is a steppingstone to managing directorship. For 1988, Salomon added two more women managing directors and six female directors. And, in 1987 Goldman,

7

Sachs & Co., the largest investment house in the United States still clinging to private ownership, made Jeanette Loeb a partner, the first and only woman among 106 people who held that title at the firm. Goldman's announcement came as a bigger surprise than any of the others: a senior partner had been widely quoted in the business press a couple of years earlier as predicting, apparently in earnest, that the firm might start to consider appointing a woman partner in, oh, another decade or so.

That there should be a handful of women at the highest levels of the investment banking industry scarcely seems remarkable— except that, until the late seventies, the only women most investment firms hired in any numbers were secretaries. "Wall Street has been absolutely the last bastion of male supremacy," observes Muriel "Mickey" Siebert, a former New York State banking superintendent who runs her own brokerage firm. In 1967, she was the first woman to buy a seat on the New York Stock Exchange. That move made the male-female ratio there a daunting 1,365 to 1, and turned her into an overnight celebrity. "In the first year I was on the Exchange," she recalls, "hundreds of women came to see me. It seemed as though every woman in the world who wanted a job on Wall Street walked into my office. And so did every woman whose husband had died and left her a lot of money she didn't know how to invest. That got me thinking about how totally in the dark women were, in those days, about finance."

Out of curiosity, Mickey made up a questionnaire and sent it to hundreds of four-year colleges around the country, asking how many women were enrolled in business- or finance-related courses. "Well, you wouldn't believe the answers that came back," she says, shaking her head. "The dean of one fairly typical school wrote that finance 'is not a proper subject for girls.' "

Unfortunately for women who were interested anyway, most of the men who were running things on Wall Street—and their clients too—agreed with the dean. "Young women who arrived here in the eighties just cannot imagine what it used to be like," says Patricia Douglas, who started working at Lehman Brothers, as it was called in that premerger epoch, in 1976 and became one of the firm's first two female partners, running the commercial-paper department, some years later. "When I was first interviewed for jobs, I met a managing director at one major firm who said, 'Oh, honey, you're much too pretty to work here.' He never even looked at my résumé." Such encounters were commonplace. Another female financier, who prefers not to be named, remembers a Wall Street job interviewer in the mid-seventies who asked her, "Why do you want to do this? Why don't you try getting a job at, say, Bloomingdale's?"

Even if they managed to get through the door, women in those days frequently found themselves shut out of important meetings with clients, because the gatherings routinely took place in private all-male clubs. For portfolio manager Kristin Gamble, one incident stands out in memory with particular sharpness. "In 1971 there was an important dinner with some clients that was held at the Links Club," she says, able to laugh good-naturedly about it now. "I was standing there talking to someone, with a drink in one hand and an oyster in the other, when two men who worked there—one on each side of me—removed me physically from the room. It put a pall on the whole party. As consolation they said, 'Oh, don't take this personally. We did the same thing to an ambassador's wife last week.'" Suzanne Jaffe, another longtime Wall Streeter who for two years managed New York State's $24 billion pension fund, can recall plenty of similar scenes from the seventies. "I was thrown out of all the best clubs—the Racquet Club, the New York Athletic Club, you name it," she says with a wry smile. "And, even in 1983, you used to have to walk through the ladies' locker room at the University Club to get to the elevators. They wouldn't let you be seen in the hallways."

By the late eighties, all-male clubs were obsolete at last—but only because of pressure from New York City officials, who pointed out that local civil-rights ordinances forbade sex discrimination by clubs if they had more than four hundred members and if their premises were used for business purposes. In mid-1988, after a couple of court battles and much frothing debate, the U.S. Supreme Court settled the matter in a unanimous decision that said that male club members' constitutional right to freedom of association did not justify keeping women out.

Mickey Siebert, who had her seat on the New York Stock Exchange two decades before she could get one in the dining room of the University Club, took particular relish in declining an invitation to join the latter when membership was finally offered her. "But, for somebody young who is just coming up in the business world, to be able to join one of these clubs is super-imperative," she said. "I would expect them all to join." Some have. Others aren't so sure. Judy Hendren Mello, who runs a thriving investment company, spoke for many when she told a reporter: "I don't want to be a member of a club that doesn't really want me to be a member, or that has to be sued or legislated into it."

TO HEAR SOME WALL Street women talk, most of the major securities firms are, even now, much like the men's clubs of yore — recognizing and rewarding women only slowly and grudgingly, even when their performance equals or exceeds their male colleagues'. One female officer of a large, well-known investment bank, who asked to remain anonymous, explains: "Wall Street is an intense, competitive place. People will use anything they can against you, and not being a member of the 'in' group — that is, one of the guys — is the first thing they use. The higher you rise in the organization, the harder it is to feel you *belong.*" As one of only three senior-management women in her company, she says, "I am resigned to the fact there will probably always be an attitude in the men around me that implies, 'Hey, you weren't really invited to this party.'"

Women's persistent second-class status has sometimes seemed more pronounced at some firms than at others. Goldman, Sachs, for one, has acquired a reputation as a place where no woman intent on advancement would want to work. The trouble started in 1984, when female M.B.A. students at Stanford University complained about Goldman's recruiting techniques: an interviewer from the firm had asked whether they would be willing to have abortions in order to stay on the fast track in investment banking.

In the hue and cry that followed, a Goldman official called the Stanford *faux pas* "an appalling situation" and insisted that the recruiter's question didn't reflect any policy of the firm. But Goldman had no sooner put out that fire than sparks flew elsewhere. An anonymous group of nine frustrated women associates and officers at the firm sent a much-publicized letter to the deans of the nation's leading business schools. At Goldman, Sachs, the letter said, "compensation of the top women is a fraction of that of top men. No women are partners. No woman currently at Goldman is likely to be eligible [for partnership]. No woman speaks for the firm in any significant area of its business." The letter concluded: "Men and women graduates should be wary of accepting jobs at Goldman, Sachs. Women will be treated unfairly."

Alarmed by so much hostile publicity, Goldman went out of its way to reassure its female employees. The firm threw a lavish women-only bash at Manhattan's trendy Water Club in the summer of 1986, and launched a conscientious internal research effort to find out just how angry female professionals in the firm really were. "They've asked us all kinds of questions, like 'Have you been sexually harassed in the past five years?'" confided one female vice president. "More often than not, I don't feel harassed, I just feel invisible. And frankly sometimes I'm not sure which is worse."

Goldman's efforts notwithstanding, along came a sex-discrimination suit in December of 1987. Kristine Utley, the only woman sales associate in the money-market department in Goldman's Boston office, charged that the work environment there was "hostile, intimidating, and sexist." As evidence for her claims, she produced memos that announced the arrival of new female employees —each bearing a picture of a nude pinup—and gave examples of printed joke sheets that were routinely distributed around the office. (A typical sample was a booklet called "Why Beer Is Better than a Woman," which said, "A beer doesn't get jealous when you grab another beer" and "A beer always goes down easy.") The lawsuit, which Goldman steadfastly declined to discuss, can probably do nothing to alter the high-school locker-room ambiance in Wall Street's sales and trading rooms. If, as the old saying goes, you can't legislate morality, then surely sophomoric humor is even less subject to official edict. But, regardless of its final outcome, the case gave Goldman yet another black eye.

And that makes Doris Smith's job trickier than ever. A longtime consultant who spent three years running First Boston's management-training programs, Doris was hired by Goldman, Sachs in mid-1988. As senior vice president and director of worldwide training and development, she was brought on board in part, she says, "to advise Goldman's top management on how to move into the next century—and that includes dealing with the increasing diversity of the work force, and that of course includes women." On a shelf behind her desk, she keeps a copy of a research report by the Hay Group, a respected management consulting firm. The report's conclusions, based largely on data collected by the U.S. Department of Labor, must make some people nervous. It says that by the year 2000 only 15 percent of new entrants to the U.S. work force will be white males. What then becomes of the club?

In her office at Goldman's Hanover Square headquarters, Doris Smith comes across as smart, self-possessed, thoughtful—and, given her position, unusually candid. "Do women have the same opportunities as men on Wall Street, all the way up to the top? Absolutely not. Promotion in this business generally is based on performance *up to a point.* Then, as a woman, you hit the 'glass ceiling' with a thud. Is that fair? No. Is it understandable? Yes."

She goes on: "When you consider that this business was started by a bunch of white males in the 1800s, and has been run by them ever since, you have to realize that accepting newcomers is hard for them, and takes a lot of psychological adjusting that they resent having to bother with. You know the kind of grumbling I mean: 'What is this maternity-leave crap? *I* never had maternity leave.' It isn't mature, but they are entitled to their feelings."

Moreover, despite all the bad press, some women say Goldman is really no worse than any other Wall Street firm, in its bewilderment over what to do about women. One woman in her thirties, a Harvard M.B.A. who worked for several years in corporate finance at Merrill Lynch and Goldman, Sachs, is now an executive recruiter in Manhattan. She keeps in touch with plenty of former colleagues on the Street. "I really don't understand why Goldman keeps getting singled out for negative publicity," she says. "It's unfortunate. They're a typical investment bank. In fact, they've made a lot more attempts than most others to fix what's wrong."

Indeed, some highly accomplished women at other firms admit discouragement, even bitterness, about their chances for promotion. "If I had a younger sister coming out of B-school now, I'd tell her to stay away from this business," says one high-ranking woman at a leading investment bank—*not* Goldman, Sachs, but an eminent rival—who asked that her name be left out of this. Although she has brought hundreds of millions of dollars in new business into the firm in the course of her career, she watched for too many years while younger and less productive men were promoted above her, again and again. "No matter *how* good you are, you probably won't get to the top—although the next guy to you might, and a lot sooner. So why knock yourself out? Find some other line of work."

WALL STREET, LIKE ancient Gaul, is divided into three parts. One is sales and trading, the nitty-gritty buying and selling of securities. Another is investment banking, traditionally a more genteel and gentlemanly side of the business, responsible for underwriting new stock and bond issues, acting as matchmaker in mergers and acquisitions, and masterminding the restructuring of client companies. The third part of the kingdom is made up of services, such as research and marketing, that support the first two. How readily women are accepted by their peers and bosses seems to depend, to a great degree, on which part of the empire they've chosen to invade.

The upheavals of the eighties gave rise to some ironic turn-arounds in women's fortunes. Take, for instance, marketing. Davia Temin spent a few years as the first-ever vice president of marketing at Citicorp Investment Bank—part of the push commercial banks were making into Wall Street territory—and then became vice president of marketing at the investment counseling firm of Scudder, Stevens & Clark. She recalls that "in the past, when marketing was seen as superfluous or even frivolous, it was where a lot of women got stuck. It was a backwater, a women's ghetto."

That was understandable—before the wave of government deregulation that swept Wall Street starting in the mid-seventies. With clients who stood loyally by the same investment bank for decades, or even generations, the Street paid scant attention to the task of attracting new business. But once the rules began to loosen and change, freeing investment banks to offer new gimmicks and novel enticements, the old alliances began to erode. Corporations routinely took to shopping around among banks for the best terms before they hired one to do a deal. So, suddenly, firms that sold their services aggressively could whisk business away from those that hesitated. Davia observes: "The women who were being shunted off to marketing all along are in a great position now."

Likewise in research, another field where women languished in the old days, the explosion of mergers that transformed the American corporate landscape in the eighties was a singular boon: overworked investment bankers came to lean heavily on securities analysts' knowledge of particular companies—knowledge that could, and did, prove essential in putting a fair price on a takeover candidate's head. Moreover, and more by chance than by design, women securities analysts have been concentrated in following so-called "defensive" stocks—such as shares issued by companies that make consumer goods, from cameras to cosmetics—that tend to hold up relatively well when the rest of the market stumbles. "Research was not a bad place to be when the bull market collapsed," notes Brenda Landry, a longtime analyst of photography and household-products stocks for Morgan Stanley. "We've still got a job to do."

By contrast, resistance to women in sales and trading, Wall Street's comparatively crude, pushy, and resolutely macho side, remains stiff. It can also be quite overt, as Goldman's Kristine Utley and other less litigious women traders have discovered. Apart from the tedium of constant assaults on good taste and decorum, there are many dollars at stake. Female brokers often observe that, when fat new accounts come in over the transom, male supervisors will hand them to male brokers only. "Somebody calls up and says they have $5 million to invest. The boss gives it to a guy and says, 'Here, follow up on this.' And this goes on all the time," says one young woman stockbroker, who asked not to be identified. "If I had the kind of 'help' these guys get, I'd be a multimillionaire by now."

That kind of not-so-subtle favoritism was galling enough, and costly enough, when stocks' constant upward rush made new business plentiful and relatively easy to get. In the post-Crash doldrums, brokers not only got far fewer calls from new clients, but struggled desperately to hold on to their old ones. Without much success: the Securities Industry Association estimated that brokers' total commissions dropped by more than $1 billion in the twelve months after Black Monday. So, suddenly, a little "help" from the boss was no longer just the icing—it was a big chunk of a rapidly shrinking cake. "I've still got a job, and I'm still hanging in there," said that young woman broker with a sigh, as 1988 wore to a close. "But sometimes I wonder why."

On the trading floor, women who stick it out are those who have learned to ignore their surroundings, or at least to tune out all but the essentials of the job. Ginnie Clark became the first woman equities trader at Merrill Lynch in 1977, after working at other Wall Street securities houses for eight years, and racked up a total of eighteen years as a trader before moving on in mid-1987 to manage institutional money at a small private firm. "Trading," she says, "is still a strange environment for a woman—and probably for some men, too. Besides the pace of the job itself, which is demanding enough, there's a lot of rough language, a sort of bachelor-party sensibility. But you just get used to it. Let it bounce right off."

Pay a visit to Ginnie on Merrill's trading floor, on one memorable day during the longest bull market in history, and you see what she means. She starts off the day talking on the telephone to a client who wants to buy 50,000 shares of National Semiconductor common stock. "Don't buy it yet," she says. She has to shout so he can hear. Around her, in the dingy low-ceilinged room, as long as a football field, all hell is breaking loose.

For one thing, the stock market had risen to 1,855 the day before, a record in a seemingly unstoppable string of records; the racket on the trading floor is the stamping and bellowing of a hundred bulls. For another thing, this is one of those days, known on the Street as the triple witching hour, when billions of dollars' worth of stock options, stock-index options, and futures contracts will expire. When that happens, once every three months, investors' rush to cash in makes for wild swings, both up and down, in stock prices. "I have a feeling the whole market is going lower, in fact I think it'll be down before the close," Ginnie hollers into the phone. "*That* will be when you buy National Semi, okay?" Okay. He takes her word for it. She's rarely been wrong.

On this morning, March 21, Morgan Stanley—until now one of the last privately held investment banks on Wall Street—is going public. It's yet a third cause for the more-than-usual commotion. When the symbol "MS" pops up on the gargantuan Dow Jones ticker for the first time ever, a great buzzing arises from the mass of traders huddled over their telephones, the homage of the tribe. Initially priced at $56.50 a share, the stock has opened at $70. "There are a lot of wealthy people at Morgan Stanley today," Ginnie remarks. "It's party time over there."

She doesn't have much chance to chat. Talking on a telephone with no fewer than ninety separate lines, she switches rapidly from one to another. On the desk in front of her sits a stack of yellow forms labeled BLOCK TRADING TICKET. As each buy or sell order comes in, Ginnie fills out a ticket and pushes it to one side: 79,000 shares of this, 86,100 shares of that, 62,000 shares of something else. By 9:45, the market has been open for fifteen minutes and Ginnie has written thirteen tickets.

Block trading, the buying and selling of shares in lots of 20,000 or more at a time, has become the hottest game in town. Only big institutions—banks, pension funds, insurance companies— can play, and each of them has millions riding on each day's trades. By the end of 1987, block transactions had come to account for more than 90 percent of all trading on the stock exchanges, virtually crowding out balky individual investors, who were quitting the market in droves. At the same time, the stakes got higher: The value of each day's buy and sell transactions in 1988 accounted for about 65 percent of the daily average value of big institutions' total stock holdings. In 1977, by contrast, the average was only 23 percent.

Most of Ginnie's job is "getting crosses," that is, matching up buyers with sellers. On one wall of the room a black screen about twenty feet square, like a scoreboard in a stadium, flashes the symbols and prices of the stocks Merrill Lynch clients want to buy or sell. Off to Ginnie's left, someone with a microphone keeps up a steady chant of what's available: "KLM 15,000 shares . . . 50,000 CPX to go at 34 . . . 20,000 Raytheon to buy, that's 20,000 to buy . . . 44,000 Mobil to buy . . . 180,000 Oxy, that's 180,000 . . . 30,000 Exxon . . . "

As she's talking to clients, Ginnie watches the order board and trains one ear on the voice from the loudspeaker. All around her, other traders call out names of companies and numbers of shares they have for sale or are looking to buy. She listens to them, too, and somehow picks out distinct voices in the general din. In answer to a client who wants to know what's selling, Ginnie glances at the board, listens a second, and says quickly, "Mobil, McDermott, Manny Hanny, IPC, and, it looks like, any utility in the world."

Switching to another line, she hears a trader in the next row of desks shout something about 50,000 shares of Philadelphia Electric. Ginnie jumps out of her chair. "Who's working the Philly Elec?" she yells. A hand goes up, on the far side of a bank of computer screens, and she runs around to tell its owner she has a buyer on the phone, then dashes back, scribbles a ticket for 50,000 shares, and moves on to the next call: "Look at this, PaineWebber is up a point and an eighth, it should have been up more than that by now. Don't you want to sell it?" The client tells her to go ahead and sell. Ginnie keeps a small megaphone on her desk. Shouting this sell order through it, she looks like a tensed-up cheerleader. "Don't laugh," she tells you, laughing herself. "I *need* this thing. My voice doesn't carry far enough without it."

The day is a series of lulls and frenzies. Around 10:30, things calm down a little, and Ginnie turns her attention to her Quotron screen—"our Bible," she calls it. The omnipresent Quotron—there's one on nearly every desk on Wall Street—keeps track of up-to-the-minute prices on any stocks the user is following with particular interest. "I'm checking to see whether some of these shares have hit a level where somebody may want to get out," she explains. "This is one way that having a good memory really helps. I can recall what my clients were saying to me three months ago about how high they would be willing to stay in." When nothing catches her eye on the screen, she turns in her chair to look at the Dow Jones news wire, a continuous flow of green-lit headlines and short news stories rolling along a screen on the wall beside the order board.

"In these quiet times you can be a little creative, instead of just *reacting*," she says. A little international arbitrage, perhaps: Smith-Kline's stock is down today because somebody threatened to poison the company's diet capsules. "It's only down seven-eighths of a point, here, but it dropped two-and-a-half points in Europe," Ginnie reports. "Buy it on the London Exchange, sell it here . . ."

In a minute she's reacting again, her ninety-line phone lighting up like a video game, and she's selling 20,000 shares of Ford and buying 20,000 shares of General Motors, buying, buying, selling, selling.

In a calmer moment, over drinks in an uptown restaurant, Ginnie had once said, "I wish more women would go into trading, but the atmosphere doesn't appeal to a lot of young people. Young M.B.A.s want a secretary, they want a nice quiet office with plants in it. You don't get any of that on the trading floor. In fact, when it's really busy you don't even get to go to the bathroom. That sounds ridiculous but what are you going to do? You can't tell a client, 'Gosh, while I was in the ladies' room you lost $900,000. Sorry about that.' No lunch hour, either. You eat at your desk. And talk with your mouth full." Beginning in late 1987, such frantic trading days became somewhat fewer and farther between. But, with the market even more jumpy and unpredictable than before, and upticks in share prices more likely to be short-lived, the trader's life is still tethered to the telephone and the two-minute lunch. 'Twas ever thus, and ever shall be.

While you watch Ginnie jumping from one telephone line to the next, filling out trading tickets in a frantic scrawl, the trader at the desk on her right takes the opportunity to tell you what he thinks about women on Wall Street. His name is Keith and he's about forty-five, slightly balding, in a rumpled white shirt and dark blue tie loosened at the neck. So far this morning he's been buying up Morgan Stanley shares for the Government of Singapore. At the moment he has put his feet up on his desk and begun an earnest monologue. Here is what he says:

"When I started working on the Street twenty years ago, you *never* saw women down here. Never. You never even saw one on the train down from Connecticut in the morning, and if you did, if she was standing at the back of the line, everybody would move aside to give her a seat. Not anymore." He shakes his head. He is unhappy about something, you can tell. He's working up to it. "And you never used to see them reading the *Wall Street Journal,* either. Now they do. Now they're speaking the same language as the men.

"Maybe you'll find that men's views about this differ, depending on whether they're over, oh, forty or so, or under forty. Maybe the younger guys are used to it." He pauses. He has crossed his arms on his chest, and he won't look at you. "Over forty, guys will tell you it has had a bad effect on traditions and morals and families. The pendulum has swung too far."

Ginnie leans toward him and says, "I'd *love* to hear what he's telling you over there. He's a male chauvinist from the word 'go.'" She is smiling, but a faint flush of annoyance is spreading across her cheeks. "No, I'm not," Keith says. "I have a daughter sixteen years old. She wants to come into this business, when she finishes college and so on. Fine with me. I'm a traditionalist, not a chauvinist."

He doesn't explain the difference, and you don't ask: at just this instant, you're distracted. Some evil or other has befallen the price of a stock you own, and you're trying to hear what Ginnie's saying into the phone about it. Apparently resentful at losing his audience, Keith can't resist taking a shot at somebody. "See that necklace she has on?" he says loudly to you, pointing. Above the neckline of Ginnie's emerald-green jersey dress is a shimmering gold chain with a small gold "G" dangling from it. "That 'G' doesn't stand for 'Ginnie,' " Keith says. His smile is not friendly. "It stands for 'girl.' " She ignores him.

Keith changes the subject. "For men *or* women, after you've been doing this work for a long time, you burn out. You don't care how much money you're making, you just want to get the hell *out*. Ginnie and I both know people in their forties who've died. One guy had a heart attack right on the desk." He throws an arm out to one side, gesturing toward the desk where this occurred. "I'll tell you, I've been doing this twenty-three years. Two or three more years and I'm a rumor. I'm gone." Ginnie has overheard some of this and remarks gently, "You have to have the temperament to take the swings in the market. You have to *enjoy* it." He stares at her: *Enjoy it?* Looking bewildered, he goes back to work.

O C C A S I O N A L L Y , convinced that men like Keith aren't giving them an even chance to shine, women strike out on their own. Susan Byrne, for one, started her own firm, Westwood Management, in early 1983. "On Wall Street, my experience has been that, once you've proven that you can make money, most people don't care about anything else. But sometimes the hard part is just getting the chance to *do* it," she says. As assistant treasurer at GAF Corporation, Susan invested hundreds of millions of pension-fund dollars in stocks and bonds, and she racked up an excellent record. But, when she tried to parlay it into a higher position elsewhere, she met with a cooler reception than she believes a man with the same qualifications would have gotten: "If I had been offered a partnership in an existing profitable money-management firm, I'd have taken it. But what I wanted and what the marketplace was offering were two different things. The firms I tried didn't see me the way I saw myself. Maybe because the only women they had were secretaries."

In the years that followed, Susan could very likely have gotten a fair shake from any partnership on the Street, if she had still been so inclined: Westwood Management established one of the best track records around. During the roaring eighties, the pension-fund money Westwood invested for its clients—mostly Fortune 100 companies, whose minimum stake is $15 million—earned a compound annualized return of 20.7 percent. That was a hefty 50 percent higher than the performance of the Standard & Poor's 500, a common Wall Street yardstick. Westwood's consistently strong showing, quarter after quarter, attracted a string of new clients that included Texas Instruments and Georgia-Pacific Corporation. The firm grew to manage more than $300 million in institutional money, and then added mutual funds that are open to individual investors.

One key to Westwood's preeminence has been Susan's nimbleness in switching her clients' money from stocks to bonds and back again, in order to get the best possible returns, a flexibility that contrasted with most small pension-fund-management firms' unwavering emphasis on equities. Susan describes her strategy as a matter of common sense—"I'm just an old-fashioned 'use-whatever-you-can' kind of money manager," she says—but her competitors admire her smooth moves. An erstwhile chief investment officer of Citi-corp's $36 billion investment-management group, Peter Vermilye, once told a reporter that Susan had a sounder style of investing her clients' funds than nearly any other independent portfolio manager on the Street.

Wherever she goes, Susan thinks like a professional stock picker. One of Westwood's winning investments was Reebok International Ltd., a company founded in 1895 that made track shoes for the 1924 British Olympic Team. The shoes, and the stock, came to glory in the United States with the Oscar-winning movie *Chariots of Fire*. Susan started buying Reebok shares when she noticed that "those funny little shoes with the British flags on them" kept turning up at her aerobics class: "*Everyone* suddenly was wearing them. So the obvious thing was to ask, 'Who makes those? Is it a publicly held company?' " Obvious to her, maybe. Susan invested clients' money in Reebok at about $20 a share. Within a few months, the stock had leaped above $80. As usual, she credited plain common sense: "You really can spot some great stocks just by being a little bit curious about what's going on around you. The stock market is really not as mysterious as most people think it is."

MAYBE NOT. IN OTHER precincts of Wall Street, however, people go to scrupulous lengths to keep their business as mysterious as possible. Take mergers and acquisitions. As U.S. corporations continued to swallow each other in great debt-laden gulps, the m&a departments of investment banks juggled more work than ever, with no slowdown in sight. In 1988, the value of take-overs in progress hit a record $311.4 billion—a 42 percent leap from the already huge figure, $220 billion, in the year before. The real stunner: Kohlberg Kravis Roberts & Co. won a bidding battle to take over RJR Nabisco for the record sum of $24.8 billion, by far the largest such offer in history. The deal raised the ante in the whole buyout game. Among financiers, the possibility of a $10 billion or $15 billion takeover, the stuff of pipe dreams only weeks or months before, began to seem downright reasonable.

While Congress and regulators murmured vague misgivings and pondered imposing new limits, investment bankers eyed the $700 million in fees collected by a handful of go-betweens in the Nabisco deal. "Why shouldn't it go on?" asked Eric Gleacher, head of mergers and acquisitions at Morgan Stanley. By his reckoning, banks and securities firms could quickly raise the cash to finance lots more megadeals, whose total value Gleacher predicted could exceed $250 billion.

However glittering the prizes, m&a specialists prefer to do their jobs in deep shadow, with no loose talk about the terms of any deal, and no names mentioned, period. On a raw late-autumn

afternoon at the Manhattan headquarters of a top-flight investment bank, one woman—call her Gail, although that's not her
name—is wrapped up in half a dozen mergers with an average
value of about $300 million each. "I'm working on one very big
one in particular," she says, "but of course I can't tell you what it
is. You know, m&a people are the absolute worst at cocktail parties.
Ask any of us what's new at work lately and all we can say is, 'Oh,
the same old thing.' Ninety percent of it is confidential." Even
after a forthcoming merger has been announced to the public, the
details are kept secret. "The only time we can say anything much
about any deal is after it's all over and done. And even then the
less said the better. It's considered quite bad form to talk about it,
even to one's closest friends."

As every newspaper reader knows by now, confidentiality is
imposed by law. Because mergers move stock prices, usually up,
the Securities and Exchange Commission considers knowledge of
a coming deal to be inside information that gives its possessors an
unfair edge over the rest of the investing public. The penalty for
trading on such tips? Ask Dennis Levine, Ivan Boesky, Michael
Milken, Boyd Jeffries, or any of several dozen other men fingered
by the Feds in the much-publicized wave of trading scandals that
began in the mid-eighties. Shaken by the spread of betrayal in its
ranks, the securities industry took stringent steps to spot shady
employees in advance of any wrongdoing. Almost every major firm
on the Street made drug testing a standard procedure. Some, like
Bear Stearns and Dean Witter, went further: they required all new
employees, from the mailroom to the executive committee, to take
lie-detector tests that were designed to yield a precise, neatly
inked measure of personal integrity. The U.S. Department of Labor
put an end to polygraph testing as of December 27, 1988, with a
new set of rules that restricted the use of lie detectors to certain care-
fully defined businesses, of which investment banking is not one.

"So that puts us back to the old pencil-and-paper 'honesty
tests,' " says a wistful personnel officer at a major Wall Street firm,
"and we don't know whether that works or not." He points out that

investment bankers, even before the insider-trading debacles came to light, were always painstakingly screened: "They've all had to fill out forms we get from the New York Stock Exchange and the Securities and Exchange Commission, which ask you for details on where you were and what you were doing practically every day of your life. But, even so, it seems there will always be a few dishonest people who slip through."

An intriguing question is why that slippery minority seems to include so few women. As of this writing, only two women have been implicated in any insider trading scandal anywhere. The first was Lisa Ann Jones, a trading assistant at Drexel Burnham Lambert, who was convicted on March 22, 1989, of perjury and obstruction of justice. She had lied to a federal grand jury in January of 1988, apparently to help her boss cover up an alleged illegal trading scheme. Jones was sentenced to eighteen months in a federal prison camp. In May, the SEC charged Kerry A. Hurton with having leaked inside information about a forthcoming merger in 1987. The illegal tip allegedly led a group of five investors to make stock trades that netted them $823,825.

What set both Jones and Hurton apart from other Wall Street suspects, besides their sex, was their lowly rank: Jones, age twenty-six, had never finished high school, and her position as a trading assistant was near the bottom of the Drexel hierarchy. Hurton, twenty-four, worked in the Boston office of Skadden, Arps, Slate, Meagher & Flom, a top-ranked Wall Street law firm—not as an attorney, but as a paralegal, the humblest position on the legal totem pole. Neither Jones nor Hurton bore any resemblance to the flamboyant male multimillionaires and billionaires who were similarly charged. Rather, the women—young, comparatively poor, and evidently unsophisticated—took tremendous risks for absurdly tiny rewards. Hurton's only gain from the lucrative transactions her tips inspired, the SEC found, was a loan she accepted from one of the investors involved. The amount of the loan? Just $8,500, or about 1 percent of the proceeds from the shady trades.

Among women of executive rank, no insider trading imbroglios have yet surfaced. Ask any Wall Streeter why, and you get a bemused shrug for an answer. A possible explanation, according to some, is simply that female financiers are still few and far between. Another explanation holds that women are still shut out of the kind of close-knit camaraderie that tempts men to pass each other inside tips. But that theory seems less and less plausible as professional women increase in numbers on the Street, with access to all the same confidential information their male colleagues have. Far more likely is the plain fact that women—in common with something like 99.9 percent of men on Wall Street, who have kept their hands clean—have worked so hard to get where they are that the idea of throwing it all away on an illegal windfall seems too frightening, a potentially self-defeating risk. It could also be that women, again like most of their male counterparts, are just plain honest, and have taken to heart a strict code of professional ethics.

"It's a combination of pragmatism and virtue," explains Perrin Long, a former stockbroker who has spent two decades tracking Wall Street firms for the Manhattan research firm Lipper Analytical Securities. "The vast majority of investment bankers do have a conscience, contrary to popular opinion. But remember, they also already make a whole lot of money. To risk destroying your career and going to jail, just to make a little *more* money . . . well, you have to be pretty stupid to do that, and most of these people aren't that stupid."

Beyond its usefulness in keeping financiers out of hot water, secrecy in the takeover business serves other important purposes too. For one thing, it helps to keep competitors on the Street in the dark so they can't woo merger-minded clients away. It's also, more prosaically, a matter of not counting unhatched chickens. A casual reader of the business press might suppose that once a company is "in play"—Wall Street parlance for "up for grabs"—its eventual sale is all but inevitable. But only about one in five attempted mergers actually goes all the way through to completion. The rest are called off, or fought off, in mid-battle.

In this genteel jungle, where the predators wear pinstripes, women are no longer utterly unheard-of, but they are still rare birds. When the actress Sigourney Weaver played the hard-striving head of a Wall Street mergers-and-acquisitions department in the movie *Working Girl,* real-life female financiers rolled their eyes at Hollywood's exaggeration of the character's power: nobody female (and very few men, for that matter) had attained the exalted heights of, say, Eric Gleacher's job. Nonetheless Gail—as we've agreed to call her—brushes off the notion that gender is any hindrance in the day-to-day course of events. "The work is so demanding, and there's so *much* of it, that you just haven't got time to worry about whether you're wearing a suit or a dress or whether anybody minds that you're female or any of that stuff. It just isn't a factor."

Still, she admits with a puckish grin, "Sometimes it amuses me." Gail once helped hammer out a multimillion-dollar acquisition for a railroad holding company. "When I did that deal—well, railroads are such an old-line, conservative male business, and the boards of directors tend to be all old white-haired men. Going in there to give a presentation, I said to myself, 'This is one board meeting they'll sit up for.' "

They did. More precisely, they *stood* up, all courtly manners, and sat down again only when she did. Says Gail with a laugh, "Who says chivalry is dead? But once we got down to business they dropped all that 'shucks, ma'am' stuff, which was a great relief, and then everything went just fine."

Not untypically for this line of work, Gail travels at least three days a week, every week. "I'm really not in the office that much, and when I'm here I'm running to meetings, running to see clients, running all the time. I can't remember the last time I sat at my desk all day."

Today she came in at 8:15, met with a client at 8:30, then ducked into an officers' meeting at 8:45. "At 9 I had to call a client about a deal that had just cratered, and another client who was dancing around with a potential suitor. Very delicate. Two very tricky situations." By 11:30 she was in a fourth client's office. While that meeting was going on, a team of subordinates back at her office had lined up a meeting about a possible deal that would require her to pack for a quick trip to California. Over a hasty lunch, she ticks off her mental checklist: "I have to check back in with the client I just left and see how things are going—I left a team of people over there doing an analysis. Then I have to put together a different team and draw up an agenda for a client presentation on Thursday. So far all we have on that is a blank legal pad. Then at 5 I have a recruiting interview, and after that, there are two international deals I'm working on. I don't really sit down to work until about 7 in the evening."

The most taxing part of all the dashing back and forth between one client and another may be keeping straight whose deal is in which stage of completion. That takes a formidable knack for detail, not to mention a talent for diplomacy. As Gail puts it: "For the client, naturally, the merger is all-important; it's a very big moment in corporate history, and a lot is riding on it. So you may have a dozen deals going at once, but you still have to treat each one as if it were the only one—or at least, the most crucial one."

The first stage in the acquisitions Gail works on is, usually, analytical: the client and one of Gail's teams together figure out which company to buy, and arrive at a painstakingly researched estimate of what it's worth. Once a candidate has been chosen, a courtship begins, with proposals, offers, and counteroffers flying between the buyer and the target company. "If there's no meeting of the minds between the two managements, we launch a tender offer and start buying up the stock. The idea is to win over the shareholders," notes Gail, adding drily, "Tender offers have been known to persuade the target management, too."

Finally, executives and bankers from both sides sit down to haggle out terms and conditions. "That's the fun part," says Gail, with genuine glee. "The analysis is interesting, but the consummation is the kick. And the great thing is that you're always dealing with the highest level, with chief executives and directors, not some assistant comptroller somewhere. You learn a lot, seeing so many companies from the very top."

The real payoff, for Gail, is a visceral thrill. "It's hard to describe the atmosphere or the emotion of closing a big deal. There's a lot of tension, a lot of pressure, endless long nights—and *rushes* of adrenaline. It's a real adrenaline rush when you can outmaneuver the other side. I wouldn't trade this job for any other."

WALL STREET'S corporate finance departments run on adrenaline and anxiety, usually in that order—a fact that helps to explain, and even justify, salaries that might shock clients, not to mention reporters. The buzz and bustle of the business arises from a peculiar admixture of panic and exhaustion. "Working here is kind of like being an airline pilot," jokes one young investment banker. "Hours of monotony punctuated by moments of sheer terror."

During the dizzying days of 1982 through '87, survival came to require swallowing sacrifices that would make most normal people quit. Nor did the Crash do much to make life mellower for anybody on the m&a side of the business. On the contrary, as firms scrambled to cut costs by trimming thousands of jobs, they turned up the heat on the survivors. Fourteen-hour workdays, hundred-hour weeks, canceled vacations, and round-the-clock weekends are common, especially for mergers-and-acquisitions mavens. Morgan Stanley's m&a specialists, for instance, have for years been on call twenty-four hours a day; they even carry beepers. And, since they travel a lot, often as much as 70 percent of the time and often on short notice, friends and families are luxuries.

Carol Einiger, the first woman to be appointed a managing director of First Boston, spent several years in charge of both commercial-paper underwriting and the firm's capital markets group, before leaving in June of 1989 to become a managing director of Wasserstein, Perella & Co., an investment bank founded by two other First Boston alumni just sixteen months before. At First

Boston, she managed a staff of about a hundred people, and oversaw transactions another official at the firm estimated at more than $50 billion annually. Her workdays—divided between two offices, one a spartan glassed-in cubicle at the edge of First Boston's ten-thousand-square-foot trading floor (the largest private trading room in the world), the other high up in the more rarefied reaches of the building and elegantly furnished in dark polished wood and brass, with two walls of windows framing a spectacular cityscape—were "usually eleven or twelve hours long, not counting occasional dinners with clients in the evenings." Carol's husband, an executive at another Wall Street firm, has working hours as grueling as her own, and as unpredictable. "We would open our calendars on Sunday nights and talk about what the coming week would look like," she says, adding that "all we ever knew for sure was that it wouldn't be the way it looked on Sunday night."

Then there was the travel, especially during the early part of her career, before managerial responsibilities increasingly kept her in New York—a development that Carol considers a blessing. "I've been everywhere," she says. "I've been to San Francisco for lunch. And I've been to London for breakfast. It got to the point where every place looked exactly the same. One morning I landed in Ottawa and I honestly couldn't remember whether I'd been to Ottawa before." She shakes her head. "I got into this business in spite of the travel. Certainly not because of it."

Indeed, her first taste of Wall Street–style travel schedules was something of a shock. "When I was brand-new to corporate finance," she recalls, "I had to go to Dublin to see a client, with a vice president from the department. We were expected to spend two days in Ireland and I was supposed to be in Pittsburgh for another meeting the following day. But, as our meetings progressed, we were asked to spend an extra day in Dublin. So I called someone at the office in New York who was on the Pittsburgh project and told him I couldn't make it, that I was still in Ireland. And he said, 'No, you don't understand. You *will be* in

Pittsburgh.'" She pauses. "So I was." She got off one plane in New York at 1 a.m. and caught a flight to Pittsburgh at 7:30 the same morning.

This explosion of activity has been building since the late seventies. It was made possible, and perhaps inevitable, by the stripping away of many long standing government restrictions on the financial markets. Starting with the end of fixed brokerage commissions on May 1, 1975, deregulation forced Wall Street firms to compete against each other with an unprecedented ferocity. "Wall Street has turned from being a genteel sort of country club into a very opportunistic, cut-throat marketplace," notes Ellen Lee, an investment banker at Ernst & Co. "It definitely accelerated about 1978. Suddenly you could go to bed at night thinking you had fifteen clients and wake up the next morning to find out that each one of them had just done three different deals with three different competitors of yours. It was never like that before."

Ever more sophisticated technology has played a major part in the sea change. Computers allowed daily trading volume on the New York Stock Exchange, for instance, to grow tenfold in less than ten years. "What happened is, since the ability exists to do so much more so much faster, the expectation follows," says Karen Robards, a former principal in corporate finance at Morgan Stanley who started her own firm, Robards & Co., in mid-1987. "And so the lifestyle has gradually gotten tougher. And tougher. And tougher."

With the stepped-up pace have come greater opportunities as well. In their rush to outsmart and outsell each other, Wall Street firms have come up with a mind-boggling array of new financial services and products. That has been good for women and other relative newcomers. "All the new stuff—options, futures, new kinds of securities, different twists all the time—puts everyone on the same footing. It's been an equalizer," says a male equities trader at Merrill Lynch. "Since no one has any real experience with any of it, no one can say, 'Well, in *my* day we did it *this* way.'" The competitive tumult also means, according to Patricia Douglas of

Shearson Lehman Hutton, that "the bottom line is the only thing that counts anymore. If you can make money for the firm, no one cares if you're female or black or anything else. You could be *blue*, and the only question anybody would ask would be, 'How much business are you bringing in?'"

Still another effect of the deregulation of the industry has been to oblige many private partnerships to go public. Unable to keep up without huge infusions of new capital, nearly every major firm on the Street has either issued stock or sold out to a publicly held parent in the years since 1976. Many observers think that will ultimately help more women reach the top, too. "In a private company, you can do pretty much as you like. Who's going to tell the partners at Goldman, Sachs what to do?" says Brenda Landry, the Morgan Stanley photo-industry analyst. "It's exactly like an old-fashioned private club. But public companies have to be aware of public scrutiny. For example, nobody wants to have to put in their annual report to shareholders that they've been hit with a class-action suit."

As deregulation has helped open the way for women in middle management, they've returned the favor by inventing the kinds of lucrative new strategies that Wall Street firms need. In 1985 Patricia Jehle, then a young vice president of Salomon Brothers and since promoted to director, worked out a way to issue securities backed by consumers' auto loans. The scheme worked so well that others, including First Boston and GMAC, started doing it too. Only one year later, annual sales of CARs, as they're called—for Certificates of Automobile Receivables—had reached a total of $8 billion in the United States. Another woman, Ann Kaplan, a vice president in Goldman, Sachs's public-finance department, invented a new kind of bond issue that helped New York City raise enough cash to build rent-subsidized housing after federal aid for such projects dried up. The method has since been adopted by other money-starved municipalities around the country and, not incidentally, helped boost Goldman, Sachs from sixth place to second place in the municipal-bond business in just twelve months.

At First Boston, meanwhile, security analyst Maureen White found a way to help U.S. investors figure out which shares were the best buys in rapidly growing stock markets in Europe and the Far East. "So many investors were trying to figure out some kind of intelligent global strategy," she says. "But there was no systematic way to compare the relative advantages of buying, say, German chemical companies' stocks versus Swedish chemical companies' stocks." In May 1985, she began putting out a report that does just that. Called the Global Investors' Valuation Guide, it was the first of its kind on the Street, and inspired a dozen imitators.

Some imaginative schemes are cooked up by clever financiers alone in hushed offices with calculators, computers, bright ideas, and no distractions. Others, though, are hammered out amid the carnival clamor of the trading floor. Laurie Hawkes is part of the team at Salomon Brothers that started up a whole new business on the Street: the securitization of commercial real estate. Insurance companies, real-estate developers, banks, and other institutions, looking for ways to turn more of their frozen assets into cash, began selling bonds backed by the income from their office buildings in 1982. The trend picked up speed in March of 1984, when Solly did a record $970 million financing for mammoth real-estate developer Olympia & York. By the end of 1988, an official at the firm estimated that Laurie's team had completed commercial real-estate deals worth a total of $13 billion.

Waiting to see Laurie in action, you cool your heels in a stuffily appointed room just off Salomon's trading floor. With its mahogany furniture placed in a spacious semicircle on well-worn Persian carpets, with its Oriental lacquered screens and antique brass lamps, this could be a waiting room in a Park Avenue surgeon's office, or the foyer of a high-powered law firm.

At least, you might think so if not for the noise. In the wake of the stock market's dive in 1987, the gargantuan institutions that are Ginnie Clark's clients stayed in. But individual investors, disgusted with equities and looking to cut their risks, took a powder. What they bought instead: bonds, bonds, and more bonds. So, while stockbrokers up and down the Street did the *Times* crossword puzzle and fretted over lost commissions, bond traders were barraged with buy orders.

On this busy trading day, one voice over the loudspeaker sounds as insistent and weary as a late-night cab dispatcher's. It overrides all the rest: "*Okay,* we have a *new* issue here, *two* hundred million in *twenty*-year World Bank bonds at *eight* and seven-*eighths....* *Forty*-six million now, one million in retail . . . Twenty, *twenty* million in the pot, let's *go,* people, twenty million and we're done, come on, guys. . . . " The head trader claps his hands. The $200 million bond issue, the biggest one in this hectic market session, is going, going, gone in just under eight minutes. A dozen traders sprint past you from the elevators, clutching takeout lunches they'll gulp at their desks. The telephones never stop ringing; the voices keep up their steady drone.

When Laurie comes out to find you, she's practically running. Holding you by the arm, she steers you through the tightly packed maze of desks, each ringed around with green-glowing computer monitors, that covers the trading-room floor from one end to the other. At her own cluttered station in one corner, she hastily clears a place for you to sit. "This is wild, isn't it?" she says. "I have fifteen million things to do today." In this atmosphere, the remark seems no exaggeration.

In so fast-growing a field, there is still plenty of room to experiment. Dialing the phone, Laurie gives you a telegraphic explanation of a deal she's trying to do for a Texas company, Cargill Corp.: "If we can pull it off, it'll be the first of its kind ever. The deal is to play off high long-term interest rates against lower short-term rates, so we're going to float it as variable-rate paper. The difference in the spreads is two-and-a-half points, which Cargill gets to keep." Without missing a beat she ducks into a discussion on the phone about variable tender options and legal fees. Spruce in a navy blue suit, white blouse, and pearls, her short dark hair brushed back from her forehead, Laurie listens to a long soliloquy about financial disclosure. Meanwhile, several people in the eddying swarm around her desk lean over her and wave papers in her face. She glances at each one, nods, reads lips, nods again, points to one or another of the stacks of documents in front of her—and speaks into the phone, sounding so cool and concentrated that the client could hardly guess she's doing seven things at once in the middle of a maelstrom.

Hanging up, she resumes what she was telling you as though her attention had never left it. "The sticking point is, Cargill is a private company and they want to stay that way, and they're getting very nervous now about the amount of public disclosure of financial information that the SEC requires for this deal. That was George I was talking to on the phone just now. George is their lawyer. He's a pretty tough guy. Let's go get lunch, okay?"

The company cafeteria, with its glass walls looking out on the wintry mirror of New York harbor, is a short ride away on a packed elevator. Laurie sails past counters laden with salads, sandwiches, and fruit, and grabs a ginger ale and a giant cookie. "When I have time I get something from the salad bar, or soup or something," she says sheepishly. "Isn't the view great up here? Everybody who works late gets dinner free. I eat dinner here a lot. At some point today I have to work on the details of a conference we're giving up in Hartford tomorrow for Aetna. We're trying to do a tax-exempt real-estate deal for them, which would be an interesting twist because none of these deals so far has been tax-free." Leaving the cafeteria, clutching her cookie and soda, Laurie leads you down an echoing gray-painted cinder-block stairwell, past a couple of emergency fire exits. "Faster than the elevator, these stairs. Anyway, setting up this conference is taking so much *time*. My secretary sent some booklets up there that we need, but they got lost and now I hear they won't get there until Friday...."

She flies through a doorway onto a floor of offices, and tells a colleague coming the other way, "Oh, I have something for you on what we were talking about. I'll come by with it later," and then makes a beeline to her secretary's desk.

"They *got* 'em," her secretary, Regina, tells her, grinning.

"Who got what?" Laurie says.

"They got the *booklets.* Are you happy?"

"Oh, random *motion!*" Laurie yells, beaming. It is a favorite coinage of hers. She says it the way kids say, "All *right!*" Secretaries at nearby desks look up, startled. "Fantastic. But look, we have to cancel that helicopter tomorrow because it can't get here until eight-thirty, we'll never get to Hartford by nine, so everybody will just have to drive. So tell everybody they're driving, okay? Thanks."

Back in the stairwell, dashing down three flights, you begin to wish you had worn running shoes. The next stop is a small office in the municipal finance department, where Frank Taylor, a former colleague of Laurie's, is just starting a three-way conference call. Before she switched to securitizing real estate, Laurie had spent five years underwriting bonds for nonprofit hospitals. Now one hospital group, run by the University of Michigan, wants to refinance a $12 million bond issue. Laurie, because she's worked with the client before and knows the deal, is helping out.

During an intricate discussion of master trust indentures and loan documentation, Laurie listens to Frank, talks to the client, and polishes off the ginger ale and the cookie. The window of this office frames one tower of the World Trade Center, white against a depthless cobalt-blue sky, a view as stark and pristine as a photorealist painting. When the client's spectral Midwestern-accented voice asks a question, his uncertainty drifting out of the speaker phone across Frank's desk, Laurie answers with a comfortable rattle of legalese. Impressed, the client says, "You know, you ought to be a lawyer." Laurie laughs: "My next job." "Yeah, she's going to law school at night; we don't give her enough to do around here," cracks Frank. She pulls the plastic cap off her Bic pen and throws it at him.

Laurie's boss, Richard Malconian, is a spare, balding, bespectacled man in his mid-thirties. A managing director, he persuaded her to make the move from public finance to real-estate deals. He calls her Smiley. When her meeting with Frank is over, Laurie breezes into Malconian's office. "Hello, Smiley," he says. They bicker briefly about how to get to Hartford tomorrow, and decide they'll meet at a McDonald's in Greenwich, Connecticut, at 7 a.m. and drive up from there. "Anybody who thinks this business is glamorous is crazy," Malconian says. "My life is like a Woody Allen movie."

At about four o'clock, clattering down the stairs again, back to the din of the trading floor, Laurie is thinking aloud about the rest of the day: some phone calls she needs to make, a meeting with Equitable Life about a deal to securitize the Bank of Boston Building, then another meeting with . . . No sooner does she reach her desk than an irate co-worker, an aggressively clean-cut youngish man, strides over: "About this Hartford thing, I got a message I hope I don't understand." He's talking about the canceled helicopter. For the first time today, Laurie's enthusiasm starts to fray. She sighs. "I'm getting a little tired of playing traffic cop here." Nevertheless, she gets on the phone to find out whether it's too late to reserve a helicopter, so anyone who doesn't have to be up in Hartford first thing in the morning—a group that does not include her—can fly if he wants to. Random *motion*.

"I found this pace exhausting at first," Laurie says, snatching up some folders full of papers from her desk and heading toward the stairs again. "I guess I got used to it. In fact, I usually enjoy it a lot. See you later, call me, okay? We can sit down and *talk*. 'Bye!" She's gone.

In a more tranquil encounter, Laurie had said she thinks that— far from facing flak for being female—her peer group of Wall Street women, who arrived here as freshly minted M.B.A.s in the early to mid-eighties, may have gained something of an edge over their male peers. That's because women are still unusual enough to stand out in clients' minds: "They remember you—probably because they were a *little* bit surprised to see you. Another advantage is that sometimes male clients are more willing to discuss problems with you, things they're concerned about, aspects of a deal that maybe they don't understand too well. They tend to be less defensive and ego-involved than they would be if they were talking to another man. So you can develop a kind of personal rapport that cements the professional relationship.

"And there is no point making an issue out of being a woman. Take the question of who pays for lunch, for instance. Last week we had some clients in from the Southwest, and I could tell they would be uncomfortable if I sat there and paid the tab. So I took care of it on my way to the ladies' room. The check never even made it to the table." She grins. "It doesn't do any good to confront a client with an awkward situation."

A M O N G T H E M O S T remarkable innovators in the business is Shearson Lehman Hutton's Elaine Garzarelli. Her prescience in seeing the Crash of 1987 coming in time to pull her clients out from under it was no fluke: she had already correctly predicted the start of the bull market five months ahead of time, in April of 1982, and had further foreseen with near-perfect accuracy which stocks would soar even higher than the Dow. "I've never made a bad call, actually," she said, with a little smile, back in 1986. At the time, it wasn't so much a boast as a plain statement of fact. In late 1987, the accounting firm of Coopers & Lybrand audited Elaine's predictions, comparing them with what later came to pass, and certified that she had correctly spotted every peak and valley in the stock market since early 1980.

To spread the word, Elaine and her two assistants put out a monthly report, stuffed with charts, graphs, and tables. In its fifty photocopied pages, thirteen statistical indicators—from the current level of so-called free reserves of the U.S. banking system, to shifts in long-term interest rates, to the aggregate year-to-year change in earnings-per-share among the S&P 500—are laid out in

long columns of figures. The data are the basis for Elaine's forecasts of how sixty industry groups of stocks will perform over the
six to twelve months ahead. Most of the text, spelling out her
analysis of the numbers and pointing out significant oddities and
trends, is in Elaine's own hurried handwriting.

The *Monthly Monitor* makes entertaining reading, partly because
the tone of Elaine's comments can wander unexpectedly from the
drily technical to the warmly chatty. In one report, she rounds up
all the usual statistics, replete with such notes as: "Price-earnings
ratios can be predicted using the 30-year bond rate and profit
growth adjusted for inventory profits and capital consumption.
(See forecasts on next page)." But, since this report is coming
out in midwinter, when many of her clients are packing suntan
lotion and tennis rackets for a few days in a warm place, Elaine
also recommends that her readers "tear out or photocopy page 29
and keep it in your wallet."

Page 29 turns out to be Elaine's own mini-guide to keeping up
with the capital markets while on vacation. Her clients can "follow
the stock market in 35 seconds a day by reading this little table,"
she writes. A hand-drawn arrow points to a reproduction of the
"Key Rates" table that appears in the *New York Times* business
section. Below the table she has written out a sample thirty-five-
second interpretation of the nine interest rates listed in the table.
Then, in a box to the right, hand-labeled "Vacation Tidbits," she
gives reprints of two brief news items about vacations. One of
them says psychologists believe that taking several short holidays
is less stressful than going off on a single long vacation. The other
item gives a toll-free hotline number (800-368-3531) that world
travelers can call for updates on outbreaks of contagious diseases
in exotic locales. The last item on page 29 is a reprint of her
business card, including her direct-dial phone number.

With that exuberant little digression out of the way, Elaine
moves along, on page 30, to an analysis of the consensus among
leading economists about the future behavior of after-tax profits,

government bond rates, and the money supply. Her clients appreciate the occasional friendly flourish. They talk about how good her market forecasting is, and then invariably add that Elaine is also, well, you know, she's a lot of *fun*.

That she is. Consider, for instance, how she came to develop her system for predicting the Dow. As a senior majoring in economics at Drexel University in 1972, Elaine was so absorbed in her social life that she missed all the interviews corporate recruiters had set up on campus. So she appealed, a bit embarrassed, to the university's placement office: Could they please try to arrange something?

They did: a meeting with Roy Moore, then chief economist at the French-owned brokerage house A. G. Becker Paribas (later acquired by Merrill Lynch). He hired her then and there. Shortly afterward, Moore gave Elaine a computer—one of the few in use anywhere on Wall Street in those somnolent, pre-deregulation days—and told her, "I want you to figure out what makes the stock market go up and down." The goal was to establish the first really rational forecasting system, entirely independent of investors' whims, hunches, moods, and panics.

The search for sanity took eight years. "It took four years just to figure out what I was looking for, exactly," Elaine says now, "which turned out to be the thirteen economic indicators I still use." Becker's management nearly lost patience halfway through. "I had a staff helping me, to start with. But that was so expensive they gradually cut it down to nothing. They were ready to give up on me. So I kept going, all by myself. I worked nights, I worked weekends, I worked all the time. I was never *not* working." Elaine gives a little shuddering shrug, exhaustion recollected in tranquility. In those days, she lived on Snickers bars: "I had desk drawers crammed with them. I think I must have been addicted to chocolate for a while there." The candy was partly a steady supply of quick energy and partly a substitute for cigarettes. For years a heavy smoker, Elaine had promised her father, when he was in an oxygen tent dying of heart disease, that she would quit. She did, despite mounting stress and worry at work, but it was traumatic. In common with many other ex-smokers, she has found that the habit insinuated itself into her subconscious, so that she dreams about it still. In her dreams, she lights one cigarette after another.

By 1979, Elaine had come up with a forecasting method that worked, and she was ready to cut loose a little. She still worked ten-hour days, and she also signed up for night school, pursuing a Ph.D. in economics at New York University. But she took a weekend off every now and then. "And," she says, grinning, "those were the disco days. I'd work or go to class until eleven o'clock at night, and then go crazy on the dance floor until one or two in the morning. I did that two or three times a week. It was a great release of tension, and great exercise." She later switched to running three miles a day.

The "disco days" also marked Elaine's entry into the more public side of the analyst's profession. To sell prospective clients on her statistical forecasting system, she gave hundreds of speeches. Accustomed to working alone, under the disinterested gaze of a computer screen, Elaine was at first "a nervous wreck," she says, in front of large groups of money managers. Her most effective marketing was one on one. "You just wouldn't believe how men doubt that a woman can do anything with numbers," she says. "I had to take each and every one of these guys out to dinner, and just keep explaining and explaining and *explaining* what I was doing. And I'm talking about three hundred and fifty clients. So imagine three hundred and fifty dinners."

Eventually all that eating out paid off. When Elaine moved over to Shearson in 1982 her market-forecasting system had already attracted wide recognition on the Street, and the bull market crowned her with glory. The rewards have been sweet: "I'm having more fun now than ever in my life. I finally get to *enjoy* what I'm doing. I don't worry so much. I even go on vacation once in a while. And I don't have to go out to dinner anymore unless I really feel like it."

Like most top analysts, Elaine still does a fair amount of self-promotion. Her opinions turn up often in the business press, and her picture—smiling brown eyes, tousled auburn hair—once appeared on the cover of *Money* magazine. Even so, she evinces an almost academic aversion to hype. She sometimes worries aloud that she might be pushing too hard, becoming too visible. You think maybe she worries too much, and you say so: after all, everybody, especially on Wall Street, is selling something. Elaine looks shocked. The maxim known to every student of Marketing 101—"Nothing happens until somebody sells something"—has evidently never shaped her view of the world. To Elaine, "sell" is still a four-letter word.

When you visit Elaine at her office on a misty winter morning, she waves you to a chair without pausing in her conversation: she and Shearson's chief economist are comparing predictions over the speaker phone. They agree on nearly everything. Already today Elaine has met with Shearson's retail sales staff to discuss her latest *Monthly Monitor* report and explain anything in it that brokers or their clients might find puzzling. Then she spent a couple of hours with her accountant, going over her tax returns. This afternoon a reporter from *Town & Country* is coming to interview her, and tomorrow at 6:30 a.m. she's leaving for the West Coast, to meet with Shearson clients and brokers in Los Angeles, San Francisco, and San Diego. Twenty minutes from now, she'll meet with Shearson's institutional salespeople to talk about what's in the current *Monthly Monitor.*

Somehow, she has found snippets of time in which to phone about thirty clients since the market opened to let them know she is upgrading her opinion on the air-freight industry's stocks from "neutral" to "buy." Dialing yet another client's number, she remarks to you, "Federal Express has gone up half a point just since I decided to put it on the 'buy' list." When was that? "About two hours ago." She repeats that information to her client once he's come on the line, and they talk for a few minutes about

Revco and Walgreen, two drugstore chains whose shares Elaine also thinks are headed higher.

Then the client, his voice crackling out of the box on her desk, says, "So what else you buying, Elaine? I mean, what are *you* buying. On your own account." The answer: stocks of small regional brokerage companies. "Nobody pays any attention to them because they're so dinky," Elaine admits, adding, "I'm buying Moseley Hallgarten. You should too." The client is not impressed. "Moseley *Hallgarten?*" he says. "Elaine, why you buying garbage?" Elaine smiles and winks at you. "Let's just wait and see," she says. Curious, you make a mental note to keep an eye on Moseley Hallgarten, a Philadelphia-based brokerage house. Today it's selling at 3⅜. When you check it again in six weeks' time, it will have climbed to 9½.

Clearly, for all the time she spends in solitary scrutiny of her spreadsheets, her Quotron machine, and her computer printouts, Elaine has learned to love an audience. Follow her to a low-ceilinged, windowless conference room, lit with the sickly fluorescent light that is ubiquitous in Wall Street offices. Her next meeting underway, she brightens, bubbles. Around the table are fifteen somber-suited brokers who sell stocks to Shearson's weightiest institutional clients. While Elaine talks about how falling oil prices will boost earnings of companies in the twelve industry groups she is recommending this month, she's relaxed, easy, pausing now and then to chuckle at her own jokes. The brokers' faces are grim with concentration. They hunch forward in their chairs and scribble furiously on yellow lined pads.

Yet even the most respected market gurus occasionally get a taste of humble pie, and Elaine is no exception. Her mutual fund, which had come through the grisly autumn of 1987 with banners flying, stumbled badly in the twelve months *after* Black Monday. In the first eleven months of 1988, the stock market rose 22 percent from its post-Crash low, but Elaine's Sector Analysis Fund dropped 12 percent. A big part of the trouble was paradoxical: in the early part of the year, Elaine lost faith in her own statistical indicators. Nervous about the market's volatility—as who wasn't?—she stayed out of stocks even though her indicators said "buy." As a result, she missed out on a rally in the first quarter, then jumped back into equities before a brief downturn, and fled the market again right before another rally in May. "I got whipsawed," she says, "but at the time I felt I was doing rational things. And even now, if it happened again, I wouldn't trust a post-crash environment. If I were to say, 'Last time I didn't get in so this time I will,' it would probably go down."

BREATHES THERE A security analyst who has never panicked, or otherwise misjudged the market? "Of course, we're sitting in a nice quiet office, we're not right down there on the trading floor. But the ups and downs give off an intense emotional heat," says Morgan Stanley's Brenda Landry. "That's why, to do well at *anything* on the Street, you have to be highstrung. You have to be a little neurotic. An easygoing, laid-back, well-adjusted person who wants to take time to smell the flowers—well, that person is probably just not going to make it."

In a brilliant red silk blouse, she looks perfectly at home amid the teak and velvet of an opulent Indian restaurant, like a jewel that has chosen its own setting. Between swallows of mineral water, she goes on: "What people don't understand is the sacrifices. Sometimes your heart gets broken, but you can't show it. You just keep going. The pressure is horrific. You're constantly having to make split-second decisions, and your reputation is riding on them. I've actually been physically assaulted by people—once by a woman at a cocktail party who had lost money on a stock I recommended. She had to be pulled *off* of me. . . . But no one is *always* right. It's just absolutely essential to be right more often than wrong."

Brenda usually is. Each year, *Institutional Investor* magazine surveys the biggest investors in the United States—most of them money managers at banks, insurance companies, and pension funds, with billions of dollars of stock holdings—and asks them to rate Wall Street security analysts' stock picks for the year, with points for accuracy, timeliness, and all-round Street smarts. The magazine publishes the results every October, in a special issue announcing the "All-American Research Team."

At first glance, the *I.I.* poll may look like an exercise in whimsy: the whole "team" is portrayed on the magazine's cover in cartoonish caricature, and the tone of the text inside, describing the analysts' performance, is breezy. But for the contestants, the *I.I.* is anything but frivolous. Investment banks pride themselves on the number of winners they can claim; so a good showing in the *I.I.* poll can bring a dazzling year-end bonus—and, often, a juicy offer from a competing firm.

Brenda is the only analyst, at Morgan Stanley or elsewhere, who has kept turning up in the winner's circle in three separate industries, year in, year out. Her clients say that's because her grasp of numbers makes her a reliable predictor of companies' earnings and stock prices, and she's proud of that. "Most men assume women aren't good at analyzing figures," she tells you. "They should see my spreadsheets. Numbers—past earnings, cash flow, debt-equity ratios, every number you can get your hands on—are the *crux*. They are the foundation for any responsible opinion about a stock."

For most analysts, a thoroughgoing familiarity with one industry is enough to fill a sixty-hour week of travel, number crunching, and report writing; but Brenda follows three groups of stocks—photography, cosmetics, and household products. "When I got here, everybody only did one industry. But I thought that would make me myopic, that degree of specialization, and I still believe it," she says. "So I started with just photography, but when other analysts left I took over their areas too. It does get a little confusing at times. You can be on one phone talking to somebody about the market for 3M's floppy disks and on the other phone you've got somebody else with a question about Avon's perfume business. Writing a lot of reports is the best way to keep it all straight." Brenda turns out nearly a thousand pages of reports a year.

Once she's studied the numbers, Brenda likes to express her

views in flamboyant terms. In one typical instance, she stayed bullish on Polaroid shares during a long upward run, even after analysts at other firms backed off. It was a "buy" recommendation based largely on solid financial figuring, but Brenda also had this to say about Polaroid: "It is a glamour stock, and glamour means passion. There's something about Polaroid that inspires passion. At just over $50 a share, the stock is not selling on earnings or return on equity; it's selling on hope and sex appeal. It's like Coco Chanel, who still lives even though she's under the ground." Hope and sex appeal prevailed. Over the next several months, Polaroid soared to $77.50, and clients who followed Brenda's advice and stuck with it made more money on the stock than those who pulled out early.

Her research has proven profitable for deal makers, too. As constrained by confidentiality as any investment banker, analysts don't discuss the backstage maneuvers in mergers and acquisitions. But gratified clients aren't always so discreet, at least after the fact—nor have they any reason to be. The hard-fought acquisition of Revlon by Pantry Pride (since renamed the Revlon Group) might not have come off at all without Brenda's research. As a Revlon Group executive tells it, Pantry Pride hired Morgan Stanley to find an acquisition that would help the retailer to diversify out of the grocery-store business. Mergers-and-acquisitions staffers at Morgan Stanley studied several possibilities and finally suggested Revlon, and Pantry Pride agreed.

Brenda's task was, as usual, twofold. First, she kept a constant watch on the company's assets, to assure Pantry Pride that the value they saw in Revlon would still be there by the time the deal was done; and second, she did a study of what those assets would fetch if they were later to be sold off.

"The assets were worth a lot more than Michel Bergerac, Revlon's chairman at the time, told us they were. Brenda knew more than Bergerac knew—or was willing to say, at any rate—about the value of his own company, because she was looking very closely at it in the context of the whole cosmetics industry," recalls that Revlon

Group executive, who sat on Pantry Pride's side of the table during the deal. "Her assessment of the situation gave us the confidence to go ahead and keep raising our bid, from $47.50 a share to $58. So what she did was extremely important in getting the deal done." In early November of 1985, after a three-month struggle, Pantry Pride bought Revlon for $58 a share, or $1.83 billion.

It was a particularly impressive coup, considering that Brenda did much of the work from a hospital bed. In late July of the same year, she had lost a finger in an accident with an electric tree trimmer at her summer house in Water Mill, near Southampton. Trying to get to an emergency ward, she got caught in a typical Sunday-night traffic snarl on the Long Island Expressway. That delay contributed to a severe infection, and Brenda didn't get back to her office until after Labor Day. "But I had a phone and a calculator in the hospital," she says, grinning. "So I kept right on working, of course." She looks at her hands, with their nine long red nails and two hefty diamond rings, for a long moment. Then she says, "My trademark gesture used to be a certain way of running my fingers through my hair. I don't do that anymore."

Once upon a time, before deregulation swept Wall Street, flamboyance played no part in the life of analysts. They were scholars, whose job was to learn everything there was to know about a given industry and all the companies in it, and then put that knowledge into hefty written reports, stuffed with arcane detail, that would help brokers decide which stocks to recommend to clients. Analysts in those days were never expected to do anything so crass as sell their own research. In the eighties, that changed drastically. Knowledge, impartiality, and a knack for detail are still important. But these days—as Elaine, Brenda, and scores of other analysts have realized—they must sell too, staying in constant cosseting contact with money managers, and plugging their own expertise on TV programs like *Wall Street Week* and in the business press.

Unlike Elaine Garzarelli, Brenda harbors no ambivalence toward the spotlight; indeed, she gets a kick out of it: "To be good at this job, you have to be able to read subtle shifts in the market, and pay attention to a million details—but the next moment, *ta-dah!* It's show biz! You have to come across well on TV and in front of big groups of clients. You have to keep people *awake.*" Brenda knows how to do that. She is fond of the grand gesture, the outrageous remark, the hyperbolic aside. She glitters, even for an audience of one.

S O M E O F T H E Street's most perspicacious deep thinkers aren't to be found at traditional investment houses but at commercial banks. Beginning in the early eighties, major New York banks leaped headlong into businesses they'd traditionally ignored. The Glass-Steagall Act, a federal law passed in 1933, barred them from trading or underwriting stocks issued by corporations. A long and costly lobbying effort, aimed at getting Congress to repeal Glass-Steagall, moved the Federal Reserve Board in early 1989 to allow commercial banks to underwrite corporate bonds (but not stocks) as well as trade them. Heartened by that victory, Citibank, Chase Manhattan, and other giant banks kept behaving more and more like Wall Street firms. On whatever front they could, they charged into the investment-banking fray.

Investment Dealers Digest has noted, for instance, that commercial banks put together mergers and acquisitions valued at $9.3 billion in 1985, or 17.3 percent of the year's total, up from nearly nothing only a few years earlier. The proportion in the late eighties climbed to more than 25 percent. As for trading, Citibank and its ilk have long been busy buying and selling government securities. Of the thirty-five largest dealers in that $100-billion-a-day market in 1986, fourteen were commercial banks. By late 1988 they had gotten still more aggressive about it, and came to control more than one-third of the trading.

When economist Leslie Daniels arrived in New York looking for work in 1983, Chase Manhattan was already acting more like Merrill Lynch or Salomon Brothers than ever before. The bank

was in the midst of hiring a staff of economists and market strate-
gists to invent new financial instruments and find new ways to
milk the old ones. All over Wall Street, at the same time, securities
firms had also begun hiring bright academic theoreticians—known,
with reluctant admiration, as "rocket scientists"—and for the same
purpose. The thinkers' task is to use abstruse mathematical theo-
ries to stretch the profit-making possibilities of the markets. "Since
the early eighties, there has been a tremendous amount of academic
research on trading strategies and risk analysis, which you never
used to see," Leslie observes. "Wall Street and the big banks are
very receptive. We're all trying like hell to outsmart each other."

Leslie, who holds a Ph.D. in economics from Stanford, started out
at Chase as a "rocket scientist," in charge of a team of theoreticians
that was working on new hedging strategies. "It was enormously
stimulating work, and we developed some very interesting things,"
she says. "But I'm really not supposed to say what they are. Sorry."

Most toilers in the vineyards of finance, if they change jobs,
move to a different firm but stay within their original field. In
this, Leslie is an exception. After several years of abstract rumina-
tion, the rough-and-tumble of the trading floor began to intrigue
her. She decided to step down from her ivory tower into the trenches.
Leslie learned how to trade bonds, and how to manage a trading
department. She rattles off her list of wares: "Cross-market arbitrage,
U.S. governments, mortgage-backeds, agencies, municipals, zero-
coupons, and options." Every day, Leslie oversees trades worth
hundreds of millions of dollars.

She likes it, partly because the job presents "a constant stream of
intellectual challenges," she says. "Then too, trading is unlike
anything else except maybe sports, in that a score is kept. At the
end of the day you can look at your profit-and-loss numbers and
get a clear-cut, quantitative measure of precisely how you did. No
ifs, ands, or buts."

Watch her on the trading floor at Chase. In a charcoal-knit
dress, her snakeskin shoes kicked off and black hair loose over her

shoulders, Leslie is coiled in a chair with her legs tucked under her, smoking. She approaches her work with a predatory cool. Waving her hand at the dozens of desks packed in around hers, a sea of Brooks Brothers shirts, somber ties, and clean-shaven faces, Leslie remarks, "As you can see, we have all men here now. I'm trying to fix that, gradually. I just hired another back-up trader, who is a woman." She'll be the only other woman here.

This trading floor is as vast, and as claustrophobic, and as drab, as those of Salomon Brothers or Merrill Lynch, but it's much quieter. That's partly because Chase isn't allowed by law to trade stocks. Much of the cacophony on other trading floors arises from the in-house auctioning of shares, a style of trading aptly called an "open-outcry market." By contrast, these buyers and sellers of bonds get their information, and do their trades, by peering at silent computer screens and speaking in low tones into phones that blink instead of ringing. The light makes everyone look ashen.

On this day in May, moreover, the big room is particularly becalmed. After a strong surge that lasted several months, the bond market has turned cautious. "Money managers started to sell about three weeks ago, and now they're sitting back and watching," says Leslie, flicking a glossy strand of hair away from her cheek. "We've already had one correction—we're down fifty basis points, or half a percentage point, so far—and everybody's waiting for another one." A "correction" is a bit of jargon that carries an almost comical whiff of understatement. The word refers to a dive, often dizzying, in the price of something, when the price has been rising farther or faster than usual. Many a hapless trader and more than a few investors have seen their profits wiped out, and then some, by a "correction."

Leslie starts off the day buying ten-year government bonds. The buttons on her switchboard connect her directly to brokerage houses whose names—RMJ, Garban, MKI—are hardly household words. Like wholesale merchants, they act as go-betweens for gargantuan institutions, mostly banks: any bid or offer under $1 million is too small. While she's calling the brokers to find out who's bidding on what, Leslie watches her computer screens for price changes, and listens on a second phone to the flat, clipped voice of a floor broker at the Chicago Board of Trade, a major clearinghouse for futures trades. He is giving a nonstop, bid-by-bid description of what's happening in the pits there, who's bidding, who's offering, who's bowing out. "We have a position now in ninety-five different securities, *and* cash positions against them," Leslie tells you. "So we rely on him, the position clerk, to help keep track of it all." A pause, listening. She frowns, lights another cigarette, and murmurs, "Hm, futures are already down for the day."

By about ten o'clock, the bond market seems to have stalled out. Price changes are shown on the computer screens by blinking digits and, in the past forty minutes, nothing has blinked. "Okay, kids, nothing's moving, let's roll," Leslie mutters under her breath. She starts punching buttons on the phone, calling her brokers to put out sell orders, which flicker on her screen, and everyone else's, within a few seconds. "Now," she says, sitting back, "I'm just going to wait and see what happens. On days like this, you do a lot of hanging around waiting for prices to hit your level."

Whatever happens next in this nervous market, Leslie must come out at least 7 percent ahead, in hard dollars and cents, of where she started in the morning. She is trading for Chase's own account, rather than on behalf of outside clients. The hundreds of millions in her department's hands are, in effect, borrowed from Chase Manhattan Bank, at a daily "carry"—short for "carrying charge," like a rate of interest on a loan—of 6.75 percent. She's pretty sure she'll make it, as she has on every other day. She seems perfectly calm, apart from all those cigarettes, and even faintly amused.

Her eyes on the market's electronic pulse, Leslie says, thinking aloud: "A lot of games get played on the screens. Sometimes, for example, like right there"—she points to a blinking number—"something will be posted as a bid when it really isn't, it's somebody floating an offer who's hoping to attract a higher bid than he's seen so far. A decoy, if you will. Part of learning how to trade is figuring out how to recognize this sort of thing. Brokers can be very helpful." She grins. "The main thing is always to know who's doing what to whom."

As a manager, Leslie has a heap of paperwork to keep up with. All through the morning, people stop by and dump papers on her desk—mail, memos, forms to fill out, reports to sign. At one point she fishes around in her wastebasket to find something important that she threw away an hour ago. "I'm very impulsive about throwing things out," she says, her voice coming up muffled from under her desk. "It's my worst fault." Sitting up, she gestures at the growing stack of stuff on her desk and adds, "But otherwise it just piles *up*. I can't get to any of it until after the market closes." With a little sigh, she turns her attention to the Dow Jones news-wire headlines sliding across one of her computer monitors. A high-ranking official of the Federal Reserve Board is giving a speech this morning, one news item says. Whatever is in it, about interest rates, the money supply, or the Fed's predictions for inflation over the next few years, could have an impact on bond prices.

While she's watching, Leslie picks up a call from her broker at Garban, listens for a few seconds, and answers, "Nope, I'll pass on that, thanks." Smiling, she hangs up. "They've got somebody who wants to swap me Augie 85s for May 85s. Even." She means a one-to-one trade of zero-coupon bonds; her "Augies" mature in August, while the other trader's bonds mature in May. As she's explaining to you why she turned down the trade, you picture a diagram in a textbook. "The yield curve is positive, so moving *inside* the curve from right to left—backwards in time, that is, from August to May—isn't a good idea for me.

"But . . . " Leslie breathes a plume of smoke and speaks lightly, suddenly as playfully pleased as a precocious child with a birthday coming up, "that is very valuable information, anyway. Because now I know that this guy, this particular trader, is short in these zeros. And he needs them to meet his margins. So I am a happy girl, because all I have to do is wait—" she crushes out her cigarette with a shrewd little smile "—and there is a nice offer, and a nice profit, right around the corner."

As placid as she now seems, Leslie admits that the switch from theorizing to trading was a bit bumpy. "It's one thing to know the products and do the math analysis, but to be out there on the firing line . . . Until you get used to it, it's very frightening. A big part of it is just getting comfortable with the language. The terms are very precise." One common mistake new traders make is to end up selling something they meant to buy, and vice versa: "The two most important words are 'for' and 'at.' For instance, if you say, 'I'm a ten bid for five bonds,' you're buying. If you say, 'Bid five bonds at ten,' you're selling. You have, say, $20 million at stake, and about one-tenth of a second to get it *right.*" She laughs, tapping a long ash into a plastic ashtray. "You wouldn't believe how much you sweat it, your first few days. You don't sleep at night. You *can't.*"

In this, she's hardly alone. Among people who spend their days betting millions on a rapidly changing series of tiny green numbers, most say that grace under pressure comes hard—even after years of experience. Consider, for example, the life of the currency trader. Sarah Gopher-Stevens runs the currency-trading department at Berisford Capital, a U.S. subsidiary of the British commodities giant S. W. Berisford. Most of the biggest currency-trading firms on Wall Street are British, because of London's historic dominance of the money-trading business. And many firms expanded rapidly in the eighties, on both sides of the ocean, as the currency business exploded; average daily trading volume soared, according to the Federal Reserve Bank of New York, from just under $20 billion a day in 1980 to well over $50 billion eight years later.

Drop in on Sarah at the end of a trading day and find her sitting back in her chair relaxing for the first time in seven hours, computers blank and phones finally silent. Falling through heavily tinted windows, the late-afternoon light in the long, hushed room is a peculiar dusky violet, like the light in an aquarium. A few desks away, a little group of men tally up their trades for the day and talk about their lawns. One trader knows a foolproof way of getting rid of dandelions. Another keeps saying, "But I *like* dandelions. I like the way they look. What's so terrible about dandelions? What did a dandelion ever do to you?"

Sarah sighs, stretches her arms over her head, and settles down to her calculator. On an average day, she buys and sells about $60 million worth of Deutschmarks, yen, Swiss francs, and other currencies. But today was a little slow because of a bank holiday in London, and her trades came to only $15 million. "I like busy days much better," she says. "On a really fast-moving day, your juices are flowing, you can feel your adrenaline running, running. It's more exciting than anything else I can think of."

Still, when she describes what she does, it's clear the excitement is charged with a heavy dose of dread. "You sit here and you can be down a lot of money. You feel the pain. A bad position sticks in your mind, and it influences the way you trade, so that you can get overly cautious and miss some good opportunities.

"Earlier today I was long in Deutschmarks. The dollar kept going higher, and the Deutschmark went lower—substantially lower. I decided to hold on and see what would happen. I was feeling very ambivalent about the market, the direction of it. When a position goes against you, when you're holding something that's falling, it feels the *worst* just before it starts to come back. So you could easily say, 'Let me get out now and take the loss before it gets any worse.' Many times you get this sinking feeling just before it starts turning. If everybody feels that way at once, they all sell at once, and then there is a moment when there are no more sellers! And of course then it goes up again.

"If you have sold at that low point when everybody else is selling, you *hate* yourself as a trader, you don't trust your own judgment anymore, and you can get so pissed off that it makes you mess up other trades.

"So it's important not to get too emotional. Not to let your ego get in the way. Otherwise you say to yourself, 'Oh Lord, I just lost $100,000. I have to get it back right away.' So you rush in and do something arbitrary. And you lose again."

AT LEAST ANALYSTS and traders, along with most other corporate-finance specialists, enjoy a degree of privacy. Their quotidian triumphs and tailspins are usually known only to themselves, their colleagues, their bosses, their clients. It's a relatively small and sympathetic world. By contrast, one group of Wall Streeters must try to appease a far larger and more imponderable audience—an audience of people who have what they would describe as *real* jobs, in the real world of subways and freeways and bills to pay and kids to raise. An audience of people who wouldn't know a tax-loss carry-forward or a sinking-fund debenture if it walked up and bit them on the arm. These people ride the subways of New York; they read the *Post* or the *Daily News;* they buy lottery tickets; they are, in short, real Americans. And they have no patience for complicated explanations of complicated situations.

So you better have something to say. And it better be good. And it better be simple.

Accommodating this crowd is the domain of Wall Street's public-finance departments. State and city governments need huge amounts of money to keep running, and much of that cash does not—and by the evidence will not—come from taxpayers. No, it comes from investors, people who buy bonds. A great many hospitals, schools, reservoirs, highways, and prisons out there in the heartland, in Missouri and Pennsylvania, in Indiana and Wyoming, originate one way or another in downtown Manhattan.

It all starts with the public-finance departments of Wall Street firms, which work out complicated fund-raising schemes in cooperation with government officials. And it takes a special kind of person to go *into* this line of work: who in her right mind wants to see her best prognosticating splashed, in greatly distorted form, all over the front page of the New York *Post?*

Not surprisingly, in the late seventies and early eighties, eager young fast-trackers in august investment-banking firms dodged public finance in favor of corporate deal making. C. Austin Fitts was tempted to join the majority. "Doing municipal bond issues was important, sure. Okay, fine, people need housing, they need schools, they need hospitals. And municipal bonds raise the funds for all that, so you could feel virtuous doing it," she recalls. "But, by comparison with corporate finance, it seemed *dull.* And the prestige was so low. Good people just stayed away in droves. I mean the smartest people just *ran.*"

Well, maybe not all the smartest people.

Picture young Austin Fitts. When she arrived at Dillon, Read in the late seventies, New York City had just come out of its near-suicidal fiscal nosedive and was ready to start borrowing again. As a young associate, Austin helped put together the city's first post-crisis bond issue. "I did not want to go into public finance. But it seemed to me then that state and local governments were in trouble, and they needed all kinds of good help," she says. Help that, in the ordinary scheme of things, they couldn't afford. Exxon or IBM or Procter & Gamble can hire legions of accountants, analysts, financial wizards, talent galore. A new elementary school, or a sewage-treatment plant, or a badly needed bridge — these were things it took scarce talent and ingenuity to figure out how to pay for. Even in those days, it took money to raise money. Brains and expertise are expensive.

As it happened, the Reagan years would make state and local public projects still more barefoot and bereft than they had been before. The need for Wall Street intervention was about to become severe. But nobody knew that yet, and Austin perhaps least of all. "I looked around," she says. "And I saw how things were going. And I said to myself: 'If an ounce of sweat will get you farther in public finance, then that's the way to go.'"

Most of her career ever since has been spent bailing New York City, and other impecunious towns, out of very deep trouble. "In some ways, public finance is more complex than corporate finance," she notes. "When you work with cities and states instead of with corporations, you get mixed up in political storms of one kind or another, which can really be crazy.

"When we did the first big financing for the subway system, for instance, we had to figure out whether subway fares alone could support the system if the economy got worse—if, say in ten years' time, inflation were to climb to double digits and the prime rate were at 14 percent and so on. It was a real doomsday scenario, *extremely* unlikely, *entirely* hypothetical. But we had to know. The answer we came up with was, yes, subway riders could support the system, and pay the bondholders, without any federal or state aid, and the fare—which was 75 cents at that time—would be $3. Of course, under those economic conditions a quart of milk would cost $3 too."

Naturally, the New York *Post* ran a giant front-page headline: SUBWAY FARE TO GO TO $3. Austin describes the next few days as "pandemonium. Our phones were ringing off the hook; we couldn't answer the phones fast enough. It took a few weeks to straighten out the confusion.

"People in corporate finance are aghast at these kinds of things. It's really quite different from anything that most corporations usually have to deal with," Austin observes. "But voters do have a right to know what's going on. And I like living in a political system where the public forums get out of hand now and then. It certainly makes my job livelier."

In late 1985, Austin was named the first woman partner of Dillon, Read, one of the Street's oldest and most august firms, and one of the last privately owned. Adept at finding ingenious ways to keep New York afloat, she was hailed by *BusinessWeek* as "The Wonder Woman of Muni Bonds." Even as the Reagan Administration and Congress sent their confused messages—slashing federal support for municipalities and states, while undermining private funds by changing the rules so that many government bonds became less appealing to investors—Austin's efforts made Dillon, Read one of the fastest-growing underwriters of municipal securities in the United States.

Over lunch in a fashionable midtown restaurant, Austin says she believes that men and women on the Street are becoming more and more equal. "Not that many years ago, if they'd hire a woman at all, guys would hire the kind of woman they'd want to fix their younger brother up with—you know, pretty and very sweet but maybe not too awfully bright, or too aggressive. Certainly not the kind of person they'd want trading their bond portfolio," she remembers. "Meanwhile, young tigers who happened to be women were going begging. That isn't happening so much anymore. The Street has gotten so competitive you just need the very best people you can get, male or female or *whatever.*" Austin, whose first name is Catherine, smiles at the suggestion that she uses Austin, her middle name, for business reasons. "People always assume that, but no. I started using Austin in high school, because everybody kept calling me Cathy, and I didn't like the name Cathy. Believe me, in those days I didn't know what a bond was."

She wraps a silk scarf around her neck, mentally adding up the figures on the lunch check, and reflects, "One of the dangers of being a woman on Wall Street is that you don't always get the same feedback a man would get. If you're a 'girl,' men hesitate to yell at you if you do something stupid. And sometimes the only way to learn is by getting yelled at. So I always sought out people to work for who would yell at me. People that nobody else wanted to work for, because they were known as screamers. And I'm tough on the young women who work for me now.

"Women's push for success has yet to be fought out on the partner level, the highest level. There are still so few women partners or managing directors." She reflects for a minute, absent-mindedly smoothing the linen tablecloth with long, manicured fingers, and then declares: "It won't be long now before being a woman is *completely* a nonissue. I can see it coming now. And I'll tell you why." With a mischievous look, conspiratorial, she leans forward a little, folding her arms on the edge of the table. "*Because* —" a short pause, for effect—"all these men in their fifties who've been running things for years? Well, now almost every one of them has a young, ambitious daughter, maybe in college, maybe already in business school. Everyone wants to see his daughter succeed and make money. So suddenly, you there, the investment banker with the skirt on"—a delighted smile breaks out across Austin's face—"suddenly, you don't seem so odd after all."

UNQUESTIONABLY, throughout the exhilarating eighties, more of those ambitious daughters were attracted to Wall Street with each passing year; and, notwithstanding the stock market's fall from grace, most of them are still around. Investment banks' statistics on their own female employees aren't illuminating, because most firms either don't keep the figures up to date or won't release them, but it's clear to even the most casual observer that the Street's cushy offices and crude trading rooms are peppered with many more female faces than were ever in evidence before 1980. Nicholas Crispi, a partner in Crispi, Wagner & Co., a New York executive recruiting firm, began counting Wall Street women in 1972. Then they held fewer than 5 percent of all professional positions in securities firms and investment banks. By 1987, by his reckoning, that had increased fivefold to just over 25 percent, and the proportion was still rising.

One sign of women's increasing presence at the entry level of the money business has been the flourishing of the Financial Women's Association of New York. It started in the mid-fifties with only eight members. Joan Williams Farr, one of those founders, explains: "We were very young, in our early twenties, and we all worked in organizations where we were the only female professionals. We didn't know any other women in finance, and so we just wanted to have lunch together once in a while. It was a kind of primitive networking." By its thirtieth birthday FWANY had grown to 350 members. Along the way it had become a full-fledged nonprofit professional organization, with a full-time staff, a busy program of seminars, a monthly newsletter, a bevy of committees, and a scholarship fund.

Myrna Weiss, another of the original eight FWANY members, believes that the ever-larger numbers of young women who came to Wall Street in the eighties were the first ones to enjoy real equality. "These young men and women have already been working side by side and studying side by side for years. It comes naturally now, compared to how it was years ago," she observes. "In fact, I've noticed a trend lately: people seem to be marrying their business-school sweethearts."

Among the hordes of M.B.A.s who hit the Street while the bull ran, men and women did seem to take an easy camaraderie as a matter of course. One typical mid-eighties batch of trainees at Salomon Brothers, for instance, included a woman who was pregnant throughout the program. The men in the group set up betting pools and put wagers on when the baby would be born and how much it would weigh. "These guys are great, they'll bet on anything," fellow trainee Joanne Tillemans remarked at the time.

Follow Joanne through a day of Salomon's training program, and you see what fresh arrivals to Wall Street face. From the look of it, this could be any college classroom in America. The students, though, are dressed in impeccable suits, and they all seem a little edgy. About 130 chairs—the familiar college lecture-hall kind whose broad right arms will support elbows, notebooks, and coffee cups— are arranged on ascending tiers that face a gigantic blackboard at the front of the room. Off to one side of the board is a makeshift coffee bar, three enormous cafeteria-style urns on plastic tables. The students straggle in, glancing around at the briefcases and papers and jackets they scattered over the room in an earlier session, and queue up for coffee. Some are talking loudly about their weekends. In a couple of minutes the coffee has run out. Several people make tea with four bags to a paper cup—"for the horsepower," one remarks—and somebody asks somebody else about a party. "It was great," the answer comes back, tossed over a crisp white-shirted shoulder. "Quieter than the last one. We only got three complaints." A pause, then casually: "Blew out a couple of speakers, though."

The teacher, a short, nattily dressed man in his early forties, wearing horn-rimmed glasses, comes in as the class is settling down. He has to stretch to write, in a small, precise hand, all capitals, along the top edge of the enormous blackboard: HOW THE WORLD WORKS. For the next two hours, in his extraordinarily tiny, tidy handwriting, he proceeds to cover the board with an intricate diagram, all the while explaining that the world revolves around the demand for, and supply of, credit. The federal government, trillions in debt, is the biggest glutton for credit; but corporations, state and local governments, foreign fiefdoms, empires, and democracies, and even individuals are credit-hungry too. Each group of borrowers fills up its own section of the blackboard: arrows connect them in all directions, and at the center, where arrows converge, is a circle labeled INVESTMENT BANKS.

At one point in his rapid-fire lecture, the teacher talks briefly about the deregulation of savings-and-loans in the seventies, and how the removal of interest-rate ceilings on mortgages altered the entire money marketplace forever. "I like to say—and if you live in New York, you know I'm only half joking—that, if you can pay $500 a month, there is no shortage of parking in midtown Manhattan. There is *plenty* of parking," he says. "In other words, at the right price, there is no shortage of anything." Some of his students look up from their notes and smile, a little dreamy-eyed. *At the right price . . .* They like the sound of it. *No shortage of anything . . .* Beyond the wall of windows on their right, twenty-three floors down, the Staten Island Ferry, packed with miniature people, plows across New York harbor in the sun.

The teacher here is a managing director of Salomon Brothers, and his students are brand-new M.B.A.s who are halfway through the firm's four-month training program. Later in their ten-hour day, they'll compete in high-pressure "games" aimed at testing their grasp of bidding on interest-rate futures, picking stocks, and pricing a municipal-bond issue. Morning lectures scheduled for the rest of the week have titles only a financier could love: "Risk-Controlled Arbitrage," "Mortgage Conduits and Relocation," "Overview of Asset-Liability Management." Although all Wall Street firms have such programs, Solly's has long been known as not only the most rigorous but the toughest to get into in the first place. The 127 trainees in this room were chosen from more than 6,000 applicants. Twenty-six are female.

Each day Salomon's trainees spend an hour or two on the huge, raucous trading floor. Today, after the morning lecture on how the world works, Joanne makes a quick tour of the trading desks, saying hello to people, peering at computer screens, making a few notes on a clipboard she's carrying. She wants to see which new Salomon bond issues are moving fastest, and what's happening to short-term interest rates; but she also wants to be noticed. Throughout their four months of indoctrination, the trainees are sized up by managers in all of the firm's departments. "Whether they're in class or chatting in the hallway or taking a turn answering phones on a trading desk, opinions are being formed," says James Massey, the managing director in charge of Salomon's training program. "Everything they do, at this juncture, has some effect on their future here." So does everything they see. Joanne calls the mutual scrutiny "a matchmaking process. You and a department choose each other."

At the moment, Joanne is undecided between sales and trading. To an outside observer, the difference seems slight: both jobs demand an intimate familiarity with the arcana of bond yields and prices, and both entail lots of frantic shouting on the trading floor. But, as career choices, they are quite distinct. On the one hand, trading is what Solly is best known for, and many top managers at the firm—including chairman John Gutfreund—are former traders. "So being a trader would give me a sense of being in the main flow," Joanne says, hurrying into Salomon's crowded cafeteria and grabbing a plastic tray. "And it's exciting, because the traders are the decision makers, making and losing millions on tiny changes in the market. It's like being an improvisational jazz pianist. Instantaneous switches. Make a statement and move on." Picking up a salad, Joanne smiles. "Except of course the stakes are higher.

"The hard part is that you're glued to your computer screen all day, focused on your trading position. It can be hard to let *go* of it at the end of the day and not take it home with you in your head." Salespeople, on the other hand, are burdened by a tad less tension. But since they spend their days "smiling and dialing," as their continuous round of phone calls to and from clients is often called, they need to exercise a bit more charm under pressure. "I think I'd be good at sales. But then you're always in the middle, as a salesperson, trying to please both the clients and the traders. It can get *crazy.*"

One thing Joanne is sure of: she wants to live in London. "It's a city that makes sense to me, as a permanent place to settle. It's laid out in little villages. I could picture, someday, having a little farm outside of London. With chickens and everything."

As fanciful as that may sound in this setting, it's not so unrealistic. Instantaneous electronic communications have melded financial markets around the world in ways that were never possible in calmer bygone days. Increasingly, eyes on Wall Street are turned toward London, Paris, Geneva, Tokyo, and Hong Kong; and for a few years U.S. investment banks raced to open new and bigger offices overseas.

The push toward global expansion was partly inspired by the astounding, and unprecedented, vigor of farflung stock markets. In 1986, for example, investors who bought American stocks did quite well, by and large: the Dow rose 23 percent during the year.

But those who invested in Japanese or French stocks did even better. The Nikkei, Japan's answer to the Dow, jumped 43 percent while the CAC, the main stock index on the Paris bourse, shot up by 49 percent. The Morgan Stanley Capital International Index, an annual study that measures stock-market performance around the world, reported that European and Asian share prices in 1986 rose by an average of 39 percent. Coming on the heels of a 34 percent surge the year before, the boom dazzled even the Street's most bullish international analysts.

Eager to take advantage of foreign investors' enthusiasm, American corporations began to cross the Atlantic in greater numbers. In the first six months of 1986, for instance, eleven U.S. companies had issued stock in European markets, compared with only three such issues in the entire year of 1985. At the same time, American heavyweights, including Aetna Life & Casualty, Union Pacific Corp., General Motors, and Dow Chemical, quietly floated European bond issues valued in the tens of billions. "Globalization" — the round-the-clock, round-the-world reach of the U.S. securities industry — had long been a buzzword on Wall Street. But the reality, once it arrived, seemed to take even some of the savviest financiers by surprise. In mid-1986 Alvin Shoemaker, the chairman of First Boston, confided to a reporter: "Frankly, I don't think any of us could have believed a few years ago that the growth over there would be anything like this."

Tokyo became a boom town. Wall Street firms invaded Japan in the early eighties, seeking customers for U.S. Treasury securities. They then pushed into the brokerage business as well. Early in 1986, Merrill Lynch and five other American and European securities houses bought seats on the Tokyo Stock Exchange and began bidding up the local talent: junior security analysts in Tokyo, for instance, started earning an average of $125,000 a year. By establishing themselves in the land of the rising sun, Wall Streeters hoped to capture commissions from the growing swarm of European, American, Middle Eastern, and Asian investors who had taken to snapping up Japanese stocks. In 1985, these investors bought shares worth $74 billion—a staggering *twenty-five times* the level of equity buying by foreigners that had prevailed in the late seventies.

Yet prosperity hasn't done much for Japanese women. The brightest and best-educated of them, the equivalent of Harvard or Stanford grads in the United States, are as yet kept out of Tokyo's financial houses, except for a smattering of go-getters who work as "office ladies": they do routine statistical scut work, make tea, and leave at twenty-five to get married. "The Japanese believe that any woman who isn't married by the time she's twenty-five is doomed," observes Maureen White. Before arriving at First Boston, Maureen spent two years as an economist at Nomura Securities, Japan's biggest financial firm. "It's sad. Women there are at least thirty years behind women in New York and London."

Despite the tizzy in Tokyo, and in such cities as Paris, Stockholm, Frankfurt, and even Madrid, the hottest spot on the world financial map in the mid-eighties was London—hence Joanne's enthusiasm. The City of London, the financial district, often called simply "the City," is the site of a $600-billion-a-year-plus market in exchange-traded stocks and bonds. London securities firms manage more than $600 billion in clients' assets at any given time, and many more hundreds of billions are invested by way of the City in the tax-free Eurobond market. European governments raise more money in London than in any capital on the Continent. Yet, for most of the 185-year history of the City of London, the government in effect hung a sign on the gate that read: FOREIGNERS KEEP OUT. On such a sign someone might well have scrawled: *Yanks, this means you.* Then, on February 28, 1986, London began to open up.

On that day, the London Stock Exchange—later renamed the International Stock Exchange—admitted non-British members for the first time. That meant that global leviathans like Citicorp, American Express, Hongkong & Shanghai Banking Corp., and Union Bank of Switzerland could buy up London brokerage firms in which they already held small stakes. The biggest changes, though, started eight months later. On October 27, in a wave of deregulation Londoners called "the Big Bang," fixed brokerage commissions came to an end, as did long-standing rules that had separated order-taking brokers—who had been authorized to trade on clients' behalf only—from risk-taking market makers, allowed to trade for their own profit.

The free-for-all that ensued was reminiscent, in many ways, of the shakeup that followed May Day—May 1, 1975, when fixed commissions ended in the United States, sending Wall Street firms into a frenzy of unaccustomed competition. Indeed, the City came to look and sound more like Wall Street with each passing day, and not always in ways the old guard welcomed. London's record-keeping and regulatory mechanisms creaked and groaned under the crush of new trading volumes. "Back-office problems," a Wall Street euphemism for losing track of essential records and other managerial calamities too grisly to describe, abounded. Meanwhile, insider-trading scandals, some connected to shady U.S. deals, brought public demands for tighter government controls on the business.

What Geoffrey Redman-Brown, a senior director of the British brokerage house Phillips & Drew, gleefully called "the Americanization of London" created a new class of young, career-oriented professionals—including more women, who finally rose past the steno pool. The City became a meritocracy overnight.

Wall Street securities firms, loath to miss out on any of the action, busily beefed up their London offices. Goldman, Sachs increased the staff at its branch in the City by 67 percent between 1985 and 1986, to a total of 300 people. Morgan Stanley boosted its London head count by more than half, to 460, during the same year. But Joanne's employer, Salomon Brothers, charged ahead more aggressively than any American rival. The firm had a staff of 330 in London in early 1986, an 83 percent rise from the number in 1985, and announced plans to hire or transfer 170 more people by the end of the year.

Joanne arrived in London on January 5, 1986. She had decided to sell bonds there, not trade them; and many of her clients are large Japanese banks. During one of her occasional visits to the New York office, she looks more harried and preoccupied than during her training days. The faint crease of a habitual frown has marked her brow, and she wears glasses now: her eyes are tired. Lunch is a ham-and-swiss-on-white from a nearby deli, gulped at a borrowed desk on the trading floor.

"It's a real kick in London because of all the different languages people speak. The first trick is to try and figure out what the client is *saying,*" Joanne says, her eyes darting back and forth between two computer screens that show currency exchange rates and Eurodollar futures prices around the world. The noise on all sides is a constant roar, pierced by the crackle of microphones. "The trading floor over there is exactly like this one. The lights on the phone switchboard are all blinking at once and you have the same constant barrage of information coming at you—people yelling bids and orders, people tossing paper on your desk, the head trader shouting into the microphone. . . . It's all fragmented. You have to make an instant decision by piecing it all together.

"One of the things I've been working on is figuring out how to price a Belgian floater." She's referring to bonds issued by the Belgian government that carry variable, or "floating," interest rates. "Before you can determine what the price should be, you have to learn the entire credit system of Belgium. It isn't easy to explain, especially to my mom in Minnesota. I tried to explain it to her on the phone, but I guess I lost her halfway through. She wants me to send her something so she can read about it. My grandmother thought I was working in London as a bank teller." Joanne grins. "But then I told her my salary, and she realized that couldn't be it."

Joanne swallows the last of her sandwich, crumples the paper wrapping into a ball, and lobs it into the overflowing wastebasket of the trader next to her. Stuck to the side of one of his computer terminals is a bumper sticker bearing the legend CAPITALISM KICKS ASS.

"You know," Joanne goes on, "I've become addicted to the pace. I get impatient with anything slower. I never read a whole paragraph of anything until the weekend." She smiles sidewise and adds, with a small tired sigh, "And on weekends I also sleep a lot." So far, she hasn't stepped outside the City's limits, except to sleep. And she hasn't had time even to think about raising chickens.

O N W A L L S T R E E T , as in life, change is the only certainty. True, the globalization of financial markets seems irreversible, and even likely to accelerate. Stock exchanges around the world suffered together in October of 1987. But London and Tokyo, in particular, continued even afterward to increase in size and importance. By late 1988, Tokyo alone accounted for 42 percent of the world's total volume of shares, with New York lagging behind at only 30 percent. Still, many Wall Street firms came to regret their forays overseas as too quick, too costly, and not profitable enough. A full three months before Black Monday, Salomon Brothers ran into financial trouble, partly due to its earlier expansionary zeal, and began cutting back. The effort set off a string of high-level management resignations and a shift in strategy, away from Solly's time-honored dependence on trading and toward more emphasis on investment banking—including merchant banking, a euphemism for investing the firm's own capital in taking companies private through leveraged buyouts.

All through 1988 and 1989, other investment banks endured their share of similar upheavals. First Boston decided to merge with Financière Crédit Suisse, a Swiss banking conglomerate based in London. Then, amid months of market losses and profit declines, and after a painful spate of layoffs, the firm saw the seven stars of its topnotch mergers-and-acquisitions department walk out the door to start their own venture, Wasserstein Perella & Co.—the firm Carol Einiger joined in mid-1989. Elsewhere on the Street, as the stock and bond markets rose and fell with stomach-churning unpredictability, firm after firm announced fresh batches of staff cutbacks. At the beginning of October 1987, according to the U.S. Bureau of Labor Statistics, a record-smashing 160,000 people worked on Wall Street. By mid-1988, 10,000 of them were gone, and the ax had not yet ceased to fall.

Salomon Brothers' training regimen didn't change, and the program kept its reputation as the Parris Island of Wall Street. But, as hiring of new M.B.A.s plummeted, its collegial classrooms got a lot less crowded. The 127 trainees in Joanne Tilleman's group were succeeded, in 1988, by a cohort of only 32. In this decline, Solly was hardly alone: *Corporate Financing Week* reported, in its annual survey on the subject, that no major securities firm planned to take on more than 35 M.B.A.s from the Class of '88—barely one-third of their usual eighties quota.

Yet, despite the chilly post-Crash climate, women have held the ground they gained in better days. For one thing, gender seems to have played no part in determining who got laid off and who didn't—unless sex was, for once and somewhat ironically, protective. "Staff reductions everywhere have been purely economic. The people making these decisions just looked at the numbers, not at personalities or sex or anything else," observes a partner in one prominent investment bank, reflecting the comments of many. "If anything, in fact, women and minorities may have had a little tiny advantage. All of these big firms have human-resources departments who have to worry about satisfying the Equal Employment Opportunity Commission. Given a choice, it's always less risky to lay off a white male than just about any other kind of worker."

But the real evidence that women as a group weathered the Crash could be found at the entry level of investment banks: Female M.B.A.s in 1988 signed on in far smaller numbers than before, as did the men they knew in school, but the proportion of women—a bit over 25 percent—remained the same. Moreover, some seasoned observers believe that each successive wave of women, whatever its size in absolute terms, stands a stronger chance of pushing past the "glass ceiling" that has all but closed off the highest ranks. Claudia Kelly, a former investment-banking consultant with McKinsey & Co., is a partner in the New York executive-recruiting firm Norman Broadbent International. She specializes in finding skilled high-level members for financial-services companies, including some topnotch Wall Street firms. "For women, the issue in the long run is being accepted by *men our own age* as equals. I don't expect a guy who's now fifty-nine to take me 100 percent seriously, frankly," she says. She's in her late thirties. "But a guy my own age—sure he will. He's used to it." Echoing Myrna Weiss, she adds: "And the generation of women that got to Wall Street in the eighties, and the women who are still arriving, will find that same acceptance as time goes on."

They may also find that there is strength in numbers. Ever since the first pioneers arrived in the seventies, women on Wall Street have taken care to help each other out. Sometimes the help has been no more—and no less—than a heartening example. In this connection, Muriel Siebert's name comes up more often than anyone else's. "Mickey Siebert has done great things for me, and she's never even met me," declares Susan Byrne, the portfolio manager who has staffed her own firm, Westwood Management, almost entirely with women. "I was encouraged just to know she was there. She has always been a battler, and an excellent businesswoman."

Another widely admired Wall Street veteran, Mary Wrenn, started her career as a security analyst at Merrill Lynch way back in the late fifties. For years she was the firm's only female vice president. Then, after moving from research to investment banking in 1975, she was named Merrill Lynch's first woman managing director. To at least one generation of Wall Street women, most of whom are now in their mid-thirties and well launched on their own careers, Mary Wrenn proffered savvy advice and plenty of pep talks. Michael J. Carmody, a (female) mergers-and-acquisitions specialist at Lazard Frères, got restless in research in the late seventies and relied on Wrenn for tips on how to switch over to making deals. She calls Wrenn "truly the *grande dame* of this business."

In some instances, women have been quick to warn others away from specific sticky situations. When she was new to the Street, in the mid-seventies, Shearson's Elaine Garzarelli considered taking a staff economist position at one major brokerage house—until she met Maryann Keller. A crackerjack auto-industry analyst, Keller was then in the research department at the firm Elaine was considering. "Maryann told me, 'For heaven's sake, whatever you do, *don't* go to work for so-and-so,'" Elaine recalls, referring to the firm's chief economist at the time. "I asked why not. And Maryann said, 'He'll try to make you one of his harem.' So I turned down the job." Not long afterward, the economist left his post as a result of what an official at the firm guardedly describes as "personality conflicts."

Usually, though, Wall Street women's sisterly advice is of a more general kind. One point that comes up over and over again is that, for all the glitz and sizzle that surrounded it during the bull market, the Street is and always will be a strange, tough place. It most emphatically isn't for everybody. "If you take a long, hard look at yourself, you may find that you're good at some things—say, working with numbers—but not so good at others—such as working late six nights a week," says Joyce Fensterstock, a seasoned investment banker and PaineWebber managing director. "If that's the case, don't come here, because you won't succeed. Wall Street is almost a cult phenomenon. You won't make it unless you *want this more than anything.*"

For young women who do choose a career in finance she adds: "Don't make an issue out of being female. If you don't, it's likely that nobody else will. Just come in wanting to be brilliant and wonderful at your job." Even if somebody—usually somebody male—does want to make an issue of it, Joyce and other women on the Street advise turning a deaf ear. "Don't let petty irritations get to you, because they'll drain your energy," says Judith Comeau, a top-ranked security analyst who follows defense electronics and aerospace stocks at Goldman, Sachs. "Believe me, if you get bent out of shape every time some guy calls you 'sweetheart,' you're going to be in trouble."

A widespread failing among young female newcomers to Wall Street seems to be an ingrained ladylike shyness, which is misplaced in this milieu. Sarah Gopher-Stevens, at Berisford Capital, says she has sometimes hired men instead of women because the women she interviewed weren't assertive enough. "These are strong, vocal people here. So you have to speak up and go after what you want, especially if you expect to make a career of sales or trading," she urges. "And never mind what men say about it. Otherwise you'll get lost in the shuffle." Too frequently, women are hesitant to ask questions when they don't quite understand what's going on. That is another handicap. "The *only* dumb question," says Jessica Palmer, who learned the interest-rate futures business amid the tumult of Salomon's trading floor and in 1987 became a managing director, "is the question that doesn't get asked."

Marilyn LaMarche, the first and only female managing director among forty-one people who hold that title at Lazard Frères, has had years of practice at dispensing wisdom to young women who want to succeed in business. In the early seventies she was named the first woman partner of another investment bank, Ladenburg Thalmann & Co., before moving on to a stint at Citibank. There she drew accolades from *BusinessWeek* as one of the hundred highest-achieving women in corporate America. To shine on Wall Street, she says, "You have to know how to read and write well, and you have to know how to analyze a financial statement. But more important than that: You must have humility. You must have integrity. And you must *work hard.*" She laughs a little sheepishly. "I know that sounds a little bit corny, like motherhood and apple pie. But it works."

If the male powers-that-be who so long resisted hiring women were concerned lest female investment bankers alter Wall Street's Machiavellian men's-club culture, they needn't have worried. Indeed, some veteran female financiers believe that women now fit in a little too well. Ellen Lee, who at age twenty-five became the first woman to represent a major brokerage firm on the floor of the New York Stock Exchange, is an investment banker at Ernst & Co. She seems almost defiantly "feminine," favoring—in contrast to her business-suited colleagues—soft dresses with flowery scarves and lots of gold jewelry. And she worries about women who go out of their way to bury their femaleness for the sake of their careers. "I had hoped that, when there were more women on the Street, they—we—would start to change certain things. But what's happening instead is that Wall Street is changing the women. This atmosphere is forcing them to neuterize themselves, especially the young ones just coming up out of business school. So many of them have submerged all their 'feminine' characteristics, but they aren't really good at being men, either. It's a compromise that makes people lose respect. And the sad part is that Wall Street *needs* the skills that 'feminine' women in our society have been trained to cultivate."

Paradoxically, if Ellen is right, women may have chosen exactly the wrong moment to jettison what Mother taught them. As competition for clients' business has intensified, close attention to pleasing each client, and painstakingly building a relationship with each one, have become crucial to investment-banking houses' success. And figuring out what others need or want, and then bending over backward to provide it, are skills traditionally inculcated and encouraged in girls, not boys. "Men are awful at it, generally," Ellen notes serenely. "The Street has a male-dominated personality. There's a lot of strategizing going on, but not much real planning. The attitude is, 'We'll screw you if we have to, but we aren't going to make the effort to sit down and try to think of a way to achieve the same result *without* having to.'

"I don't know what it will take to change that culture. Maybe we'll have to see a lot more women in positions of real power on Wall Street with their 'people' skills still intact. Or maybe if some of these fifty-two-year-old men marry thirty-year-old professional women"—she laughs—"and realize what they're missing at work."

Ellen, and others who agree with her, would probably view Susan Byrne's 99 percent female money-management company as an encouraging prototype. Stop by to see Susan on a Friday afternoon when the Dow has just taken a 45.75-point free fall. At her offices in a midtown skyscraper, a secretary in jeans and a sweatshirt leads you along a corridor painted pearly gray, where the words WESTWOOD MANAGEMENT, INC., in slate-gray letters, are underlined by a sharp stripe of ribbon-candy pink. Installing you in a small conference room, the secretary asks you if you want anything to drink: "We have Diet Seven-Up, Diet Coke, Diet Pepsi, seltzer . . . " Anything that promises not only caffeine but sugar too? "Coffee, sure," she says.

In a few minutes, Susan comes bounding into the room and drops into a leather chair. She's wearing khaki pants, a striped polo shirt, scruffy Reeboks and horn-rimmed glasses; two chunky diamond earrings peek out from behind her short blond hair. "I'm sorry I'm late, the market just closed, my watch is broken, and my clients are frantic," she says, out of breath. "I've been on the phone telling them, Babies, don't worry, we're *okay.*" Then she grins at you. "I don't usually dress like this. But today is Jeans Day."

Jeans Day? On Fridays, if no clients are scheduled to come by, Susan declares a Jeans Day. Her dozen employees come to work in whatever they feel like wearing, and at lunchtime the whole staff sends out for pizza. "It's a kind of family at-home day. The wonderful thing about having your own business is the creative freedom," Susan says, drinking seltzer from a can. "It's banal, everybody says it, but it's true. You get to decide everything from the design of the office to what kinds of traditions you'd like to establish. Jeans Day is a tradition."

She stops a moment, reflecting, and then goes on: "Of course, when you first start out, you're so busy worrying about whether the phones are working right and whether you have enough cash on hand to get through the month, you don't say—" her voice drops to a ponderous rumble—" 'Hmmm, what kind of corporate culture do I want to foster here?' " She takes a swig of seltzer, continues happily: "But once the functional details are settled and the bills are getting paid, you can really start to build something special.

"The culture reflects the fact that I've hired almost all women here. For one thing, we're always celebrating. Somebody aced a test at night school, or it's somebody's birthday; one of us is running in a race and the rest of us are there cheering. It's a very *cooperative* spirit around here. The most important thing is to get the job done, not who does what or who did it last time. We're not big on ego. I mean, we're as competitive as anybody, but just not among ourselves. I think women are more comfortable with that style. We talk about 'the Westwood team.' " She pauses for a long gulp of seltzer and then says, "Maybe some people would find it stifling, I don't know. But—the people here are still here."

In early 1986, Susan brought in a partner: Francine Vogler, a former managing director at Citicorp. "I get teased sometimes for having an attitude like an immigrant," Susan remarks. "Because one thing immigrants always do is, once the first one gets established, he brings in the next one, and the next one, and the next one, and the next, and the next. . . . Well, Wall Street has always welcomed immigrants. First came the Jews, then the Irish, then Italians, and now women. So, if you look at it that way, women coming to Wall Street, and helping other women to get ahead too, is just the latest expansion of a very old pattern."

With that in mind, female newcomers to the Street are inclined toward optimism. Valerie K., for one (she asked that her last name not be mentioned), graduated near the top of her class from a prestigious graduate business school in 1988, and promptly joined an eminent investment bank. "This isn't the glamour business it used to be, but there are still great opportunities here," she says. And she is undaunted by the fact that, as of late 1988, women still held only about 1 percent of Wall Street's highest-ranking jobs: "The way I see it, it's a matter of *persistence.* If we just keep turning up here, and we stick around in good times and bad, the men here will have to take notice."

Some of her more experienced, and more disillusioned, female colleagues may be doubtful, but at least one male partner in a leading investment bank thinks Valerie is probably right. He says, "The women we're seeing on the Street are exceptional human beings. They don't just seem equal to most men—they seem *better.* They're better organized. They really seem to have their lives together. And they're tough."

Then he adds, "But they're not overly aggressive, sort of overcompensating, the way they were a few years ago. Maybe they don't have to do that anymore."

At long last, clearly not.

II.

THE MEANING

OF MONEY

Cataclysmic as it seemed at the time, the Crash of 1987 marked not a headlong plunge into the abyss but an abrupt return to business as usual. Once again, as in the days before the bull began its five-year upward charge, markets resumed their old erratic random movement. Euphoria on Wall Street was displaced, not by desolation, but by confusion. A barrage of mixed signals confronted anyone trying to keep track of the Street's wobbling fortunes.

Consider just a few among many contradictions: Smarting from October's blow, individual investors stayed away from common stocks in droves. Yet, because institutions went bargain hunting and takeover stocks soared, trading volume on the New York Stock Exchange neared 180 million shares during March of 1988, or almost twice the number of shares that had changed hands in January of 1986. Some securities firms, like Merrill Lynch, saw their profits tumble by one-third or more in the months that followed the Crash. Yet First Boston bounced back from a net loss in the fourth quarter of 1987 to a second-quarter showing in 1988 that was 80 percent higher than in the same quarter a year earlier; and Morgan Stanley, against all odds, continued to report record high profits all along.

In a flurry of cost cutting, thousands of Wall Streeters lost their jobs. Yet the New York Stock Exchange reported in mid-1988 that the number of full-time stockbrokers employed by the Exchange's member firms had *risen* 7.8 percent, to a record 89,375, apparently because firms hired more brokers to try to haul in new customers, even as the closing bell tolled for staffers perceived as less essential. A few formerly robust lines of business, including municipal-bond underwriting, languished. Yet mergers and acquisitions zoomed to fresh heights, with almost $65 billion worth announced in the first two months of 1988, more than double the $32 billion in the new m&a business Wall Street picked up during the same months of 1987.

Most tellingly, in prognostications for the future, the onward-and-upward consensus of the years since 1982 gave way to an old-style dissonant chorus of conflicting views. Typically, when the stock market hit post-Crash highs in June and July of 1988, market watchers interviewed by *Fortune* predicted a long bearish hibernation for stocks, while other pundits, quizzed by the *New York Times,* claimed to hear a new bull bellowing right around the corner. In apt summation of the general bewilderment, a *Wall Street Journal* reporter dubbed 1988 "the year of living disorientedly."

Most of the men and women who conduct Wall Street's daily business survived the Crash and its immediate aftershocks with their jobs intact. Indeed, many high fliers felt themselves so invulnerable that the import of the market's freefall took a while to sink in. "So many young professionals, especially on the sales and trading side, believed the bull market would go on forever. When it ended, they literally didn't believe their eyes," recalls Doris Smith at Goldman, Sachs. She was then still in her old job at First Boston. "I went down to the trading floor the day after the

Crash to see if I could cheer anybody up—because of course I expected shock and grief and depression."

What she found instead was that First Boston's traders were having more fun than ever: "They were laughing and joking, saying things like 'How many millions did *you* lose? Hey, I can beat that!' It was still a *game*." That insouciance lasted, she says, a few weeks, "until the reality set in: this was going to hit people's pocketbooks." With more than half a trillion dollars in stock prices wiped out in the weeks between Labor Day and November 20, 1987, many Wall Streeters' personal portfolios took a battering, and year-end bonuses seemed likely to be measly or nonexistent, as in the end they were. In December, First Boston's traders could still summon a smile, but rather more queasily. One of them told a friend, "The joke around here now is, 'When you come for your bonus this year, bring your checkbook.' "

Financial setbacks, combined with the disconcerting sight of erstwhile colleagues clearing out their desks amid rumors of more layoffs to come, gave rise to a new mood, and traders weren't the only once-ebullient Wall Streeters who suddenly seemed sober and subdued. Mergers-and-acquisitions specialists, still as busy as ever, nonetheless took to speaking guardedly about the future, and spending the odd moment fiddling with their résumés—just in case. And no one, not even those record legions of stockbrokers, felt much like flashing wads of cash. Sales of New York co-op apartments in the $100,000 to $1 million price range slowed; luxury-car dealers resorted to offering discounts and rebates; and the vacation trade fell off on Caribbean islands like St. Bart's and Martinique. Manhattan's high-priced eateries, whose three- and four-figure dinner checks graced many an expense-account report in the giddy old days, were among the first to suffer lean times. One symptom: "21," that venerable and snooty pseudo club, began to *advertise specials* —a necessity, formerly unthinkable, that struck horror in the hearts of the tradition-minded all over town.

Wall Streeters' unwonted low profile altered New York's social scene in more subtle ways as well, and some said it was about time. "I started going to parties again, and it's fun," says a young Manhattan architect who had given up night life for a couple of years. "You notice that the photographers and poets and all kinds of people are coming out of the woodwork—now that there isn't always some cocky investment-banker type monopolizing the conversation."

Ah, yes. While it lasted, the stock market's long, glittering rise generated much wealth and an equal measure of arrogance. For a while, the dazzling compensation pulled down by investment bankers, traders, and arbitrageurs—the most vocal and flamboyant of whom were young and male—got so much ballyhoo in the business press that it became a sore point.

Wall Streeters are still cagey about giving out any precise figures. Their reticence is due in large part to a phenomenon known as a "golden muzzle": top management long ago sent out the word that anyone who wanted to keep making such princely money had better pipe down about it. In July of 1986, for instance, *Business Week* printed an article about the Wall Street gravy train that featured a color photo of a young Salomon Brothers banker lolling beside his swimming pool with a drink in his hand. In the caption, he seemed to be boasting about his six-figure income.

John Gutfreund, Solly's chairman, was not amused. He sent a memo to the entire professional staff, with copies of the magazine article attached. In the memo and in an irate speech to the assembled sales-and-trading and corporate-finance departments, Gutfreund said that loose talk about pay "will not be tolerated and will certainly do nothing to advance anyone's career at Salomon Brothers."

An official at Morgan Stanley, where discretion is also the better part of valor, explains it this way: "Look, this is a client business, and you don't want to flaunt in the face of the client that you're practically right out of B-school and making more money than the CEO of his whole company makes. I mean, the client might get the idea that he's being taken for a ride." He might at that.

Even with caution running high, reliable information about the general level of Wall Street salaries has never been too hard to come by. A 1985 survey by the trade publication *Corporate Financing Week* noted that the top investment banks were offering average starting salaries of between $45,000 and $55,000, along with guaranteed bonuses of up to $20,000 more, to the best candidates from top-ranked business schools. In July of 1986, a report from the Securities Industry Association, a Wall Street trade group, said that average pay in the securities industry exceeded $100,000 a year. But the SIA arrived at that figure by adding up all the salaries and bonuses of everyone in the business, from chairmen down to janitors, and then dividing the total by the head count. If the pay of support staff—secretaries, receptionists, clerks, and others—was subtracted from the aggregate so that only financiers were counted, the average would be far higher.

Indeed, John Gutfreund told the *New York Times* in March of 1986, evidently before he got fed up with the whole subject, that "making $250,000 a year would not be any surprise" for Wall Street stars who had not yet seen their thirtieth birthdays. At the time, according to the Census Bureau, average household income in the United States stood at just under $23,000 a year, or a piddling 10 percent of what some of these novice Wall Streeters were paid.

Many, of course, made much more than $250,000—even several times as much. The sheer abundance of money produced what sociologists refer to, in studies of Third World countries, as a "revolution of rising expectations." As a nation's standard of living rises, so too do dissatisfaction and unrest. The more material goods people have, according to this theory, the more they want—or persuade themselves they *need*—and the more keenly they are pained by any real or imagined deprivation. The result is often insurrection, civil war, the overthrow of kings.

The revolution of rising expectations on Wall Street yielded, at its best, a relatively harmless sort of myopia, which caused people who were fabulously wealthy by almost any reasonable standard to perceive themselves as just plain folks. Take Austin Fitts, Dillon, Read's municipal-bond maven. Way back in 1983, Austin hired a very well paid full-time housekeeper named Anthony, who is also a Cordon Bleu chef. At the time, Austin's husband, an attorney at a Wall Street law firm, resisted the idea. Austin recalls, "He said to me, 'People like us don't hire help like this.'"

You can only marvel at what he meant by "people like us." Austin's partnership at Dillon, Read was bringing in upward of $1 million a year, and her husband's own salary doubtless exceeded that of the President of the United States by a hefty margin. Still, recounting the conversation years later, Austin doesn't comment on his choice of words. It's clear that she takes his point: "People like us" means middle-class working people.

It's a modest determination to see oneself, and to be seen, as perfectly ordinary, thank you; and it is not at all uncommon on Wall Street. Extremely well-off men and women will say to you, in quite sincere surprise, "*Me?* No, no. I don't even know anybody rich. I'm just comfortable." By their lights, evidently, real prosperity is in the billions. T. Boone Pickens, the Bass brothers, Donald Trump—now, *those* guys are really doing all right.

At its worst, however, the revolution of rising expectations that swept Wall Street in the eighties lacked any such self-effacing charm. The Young Turks of finance with their lordly paychecks were frequently given to carrying on, in fact, like a noisy pack of spoiled brats. In a business where money is quite literally the be-all and end-all, where every day one bandies astronomical numbers and many-digit figures that just keep on getting bigger, and where one speaks offhandedly of a deal as being worth "only" $100 million or "only" $500 million, perspective is easily lost.

Added to that, the good life in New York is even costlier and more elusive than elsewhere: so many irresistible art auctions, so many overpaid chauffeurs, so many apartments that cost upward of $2 million, so many private elementary schools that cost more per child per year than the tuition at most American universities, so many superbly pedigreed Joneses to try to keep up with. During the bull market, it became commonplace to feel poor on $600,000 a year. That weird subliminal buzz one heard on Manhattan's Upper East Side was the constant whining of the young, overleveraged, and restless. Sherman McCoy, the beleaguered hero of Tom Wolfe's bestselling novel *The Bonfire of the Vanities,* was scarcely a caricature. He was drawn—with a pen dipped in a solution of equal parts Veuve Clicquot and battery acid—straight from life.

Nor was the gold rush only a New York trend. In London, where American and British securities firms raced to expand as markets soared around the world, the enormous sums earned by bankers still wet behind the ears startled even so staunch a free-marketeer as Prime Minister Margaret Thatcher. "Salaries in the City these days," she once remarked in an interview on the BBC, "fair make one gasp." The City of London attracted less benign attention as well. Gangs of unemployed and disenchanted young Londoners invented a sport, quite popular after dark, called "yuppie bashing." It was not pretty.

ON THIS SIDE OF the Atlantic, envy more often took the form of self-righteous alarm, an unsurprising reaction in a culture such as ours, where material wealth is at once revered and mistrusted. The *New York Times,* not for nothing this city's newspaper of record, mirrored its readers' preoccupations with ironic precision. The "Home" section featured lavish decorating schemes beyond the ken of the city's struggling middle class, and the paper's restaurant reviewers, travel writers, and advertisers clearly addressed an increasingly affluent audience. Yet all the while, arts critics and other deep thinkers wrung their hands. In one typical *Times* piece, ruminating on the popularity of the movie *Wall Street,* economist Leonard Silk suggested that "pride, a leading indicator, goeth before a fall." In linking pride to more mundane indicators like the prime lending rate and the money supply, Silk surely broke new ground, although he neglected to say how pride might be quantified, or whether anyone—the Federal Reserve Board, perhaps—ought to try regulating it.

But it was John Gross, who reviews books for the *Times,* who best conveyed the tenor of a spreading disquiet. In entertainments like Caryl Churchill's strident play *Serious Money,* Gross wrote, the conviction lurked that, "with the ascendance of a new generation, we are up against something the world has never quite seen before: not just any old greed, but postmodern greed, state-of-the-art greed."

If ambivalence about Wall Street's frenetic runaway prosperity had been confined to mutterings from underpaid journalists and antimaterialistic readers of the arts pages, it would scarcely be worth remarking. But powerful and contradictory feelings about money, about making money and spending money, have haunted another group as well—a group that is directly involved and hence far better qualified, if less inclined, to comment: Wall Street women.

Like so much else in women's reach for equality, the significance of money comes freighted with paradox. At first blush, financiers in skirts seem as matter-of-factly mercenary as any of their male counterparts. Ask any woman her reasons for choosing this line of work, and the stellar salaries are always high on the list. Moreover, as women have gained in both numbers and experience, some have acquired the self-confidence to insist on being paid top dollar.

Take Sarah Gopher-Stevens, the currency-trading chief at Berisford Capital. She is happy with her current job largely because she believes she is finally being paid enough. At nearly every big firm on the Street—including Salomon Brothers and Drexel Burnham Lambert, where Sarah worked before joining Berisford—a big part of everyone's compensation comes in the form of a year-end bonus. The bonuses can be generous in a good year, sometimes topping six figures. Their size depends in large part on what line of work one is in, and how the whole business has fared. In 1986, most Wall Streeters' bonuses were terrific. In 1987, for obvious reasons, almost nobody's was worth writing home about. Mergers-and-acquisitions specialists, in 1988, made out a lot better than most sales-and-trading staffers. And as for stockbrokers— "Bonus?" said one, not atypically, at year's end. "*What* bonus?"

But, beyond that, exactly how bonuses are meted out, and the reasoning behind who gets how much, is often mysterious. Individual workers in the same department, at the same firm, can— and often do—find their bonuses vary wildly. "It's highly subjective," Sarah observes. "Either someone higher up likes you and decides to take good care of you, or not. But you can't do much about it. It can be frustrating, especially when you know very well what you are adding to the firm's bottom line and your bonus just doesn't reflect that."

At Berisford, as manager and trader both, Sarah not only knows precisely how much profit she and her department kick in: she's got the clout to make sure she's paid accordingly. "You absolutely must think realistically of your contribution to the firm, enough to go after what you know you deserve," she declares.

"And," she goes on, "apart from the excitement and the challenge, the one thing that brings everybody to Wall Street in the first place is the chance to make a lot of money. There's really no sense in pretending otherwise, is there?"

Nor is there any denying that Wall Street women as a group are the best-paid female employees in the United States. Government statistics released in 1987 showed that the average American woman with a college degree earned $20,057 a year. By contrast, few of the hundreds of women at the rank of vice president or higher in any firm on Wall Street made less than ten times that.

Such dazzling compensation has the effect of imposing a special sort of "golden muzzle" on female traders and investment bankers. Although they may suspect, often with good reason, that they're being promoted more slowly or paid less generously than the men alongside whom they work, they rarely complain openly about it. Sex discrimination suits, on the rise elsewhere, are scarcer here than hens' teeth. For one thing, it's extremely difficult to prove that a woman who earns less than the man next to her is really a victim of sexism. One executive recruiter, who asked not to be quoted by name on this subject, has been filling high-paid Wall Street positions for seventeen years and has worked with more than 3,200 job candidates. "I can tell you the compensation for women *is* generally a bit lower than for men, even when their experience and talents are similar," this expert says. "What I can't tell you for sure is *why*. Pay on the Street, especially bonuses, can be kind of capricious. Hard evidence of sex discrimination would be practically impossible to get your hands on."

Even when such evidence is available, however, Wall Street salaries are high enough to discourage legal action. One woman, who contemplated suing Goldman, Sachs for sex bias a few years ago when she was repeatedly passed over for promotion despite her first-rate performance, says she went to her lawyer with documented proof that less-qualified men were being favored. The lawyer advised her not to sue. "He said I had a solid case," she recalls, "but he couldn't picture a judge or jury shedding any tears for a plaintiff who made 'only' $220,000 a year."

He had a point there. No defense attorney worth his BMW—and Goldman, Sachs, like any other securities powerhouse, can afford the very cleverest lawyers—would hesitate to hammer home the fact that, whatever real or imaginary slights she has endured, and even if a man in her position would be earning more, the plaintiff nevertheless brings home a fatter paycheck than most people will ever see except in dreams. Surely she is hardly to be counted among the downtrodden.

Where women on Wall Street part company with their male colleagues is not so much in the amount they earn as in how it affects their view of themselves. For male traders and investment bankers, career success, as measured in dollar terms, can pack powerful symbolic meanings. Wealth and its perquisites can represent, in these men's conscious and subconscious minds, an indicator of everything from intellectual acuity to prowess in bed. "On Wall Street, maybe more than anywhere else, men's egos are *totally* tied up in money," observes a female stockbroker who asked that her name not be mentioned. "I mean to the point where a financial problem even destroys a guy's sexual confidence. I don't want to be crude, but it rises and falls with the market, if you get my drift." She adds, "This is why I'd rather date people who don't work on Wall Street—especially since the Crash."

Women, on the other hand, seem more able to separate the net worth of their stock portfolios—or their trading positions, or the deals they're doing at the moment—from their personal value as human beings. The notion that "you are what you earn," accepted unthinkingly by most of their male co-workers, seems to make women more than slightly queasy. Sipping club soda in an uptown bistro while the bull market was at its pinnacle, Merrill Lynch trader Ginnie Clark said, "Look, the salaries and bonuses people are getting paid are *astronomical,* and it's kind of weird, because that has nothing to do with *reality.* It's just that right now there is an amazing amount of money around, so naturally it rains down on the people who work on the Street. It has nothing to do with what anybody is 'worth.'" Ginnie's attitude was no mere grudging case of sour grapes. As a trader, she was earning a commission of 7 cents per share. At an average of a million shares a day—well, you figure it out.

Nancy Bazelon Goldstone, a former trader who has written a book about her experiences, has a name for the macho habit of equating money with self-esteem, which she sees as almost a pathological tendency: she calls it "Trader Head." This is "a syndrome in which one's ego grows at an accelerated rate at the expense of all other personality traits," she explains. "It can take a terrible toll on your psyche and on your self-confidence, if you succumb to it.

89

Once you start thinking that the person who makes $10 million is *by definition* a better, stronger person than the one who makes $2 million, there's nothing else to fall back on."

Women do occasionally suffer from Trader Head: Goldstone confesses she fell victim to it herself. Significantly, she reacted by quitting her job. One glaring sign that most women tend toward an immunity to the Trader Head disorder is that female traders are still so scarce. During most of the eighties, when new financial instruments were being invented almost daily, and stock prices shot up to heights that bore little relation to their real value as shares of a given enterprise, Wall Street came to resemble nothing so much as a giant floating crap game. Huge fortunes were made and lost on, for instance, stock index futures, which are little more than blips on a computer screen that represent other electronic phenomena, which in turn are linked to the outside world in only the most distant and tenuous way.

At this level of abstraction, and with millions or billions of dollars at stake, women have been patently less at home than men. Even in the eighties, no trading floor on Wall Street had more than a smattering of women, and most had only one or two. To Ginnie Clark's earlier observation that young M.B.A.s yearned for "a nice quiet office with plants in it" might be added: Young female M.B.A.s, in particular, preferred research or investment banking to trading, because in those areas one's feet are more firmly planted on the solid ground of clients' actual operations, and companies' real-life assets, revenues, and profits.

Prolonged daily contact with pure money—like deep breathing in an atmosphere of pure oxygen—can induce a stomach-turning vertigo. Some people might be tempted to seize on that as a case of predictable womanly wimpiness. But it is worth bearing in mind that no less a legendary Wall Street eminence than Felix Rohatyn, of Lazard Frères, believed during the bull market that the speculative frenzy had gotten out of hand. In the mid-eighties he was often heard to grumble that Wall Street's stability, and its prosperity, were in jeopardy, and were put there by these ravening hordes of fresh-faced M.B.A.s with their unstoppable computer programs.

The few women who have become traders, and who relish the absurd spectacle of it all, seem more able than their male counterparts to see beyond the blinking lights of their little green screens. Leslie Daniels, the Chase Manhattan theorist-turned-trader, explains: "Women don't define their entire existence by how much they make. What money does buy, for us, is not self-acceptance—which we tend to get from other sources—but *security.*" Especially for a former academic like Leslie, and for the many other Wall Street women who came here from less lucrative careers, making a lot of money means never having to think twice about paying the bills, with enough left over to have some fun and still save plenty for a stormy day.

Serious money also holds out the promise of personal freedom, of one day escaping the Wall Street pressure cooker to embark on a whole new life. One female investment banker thinks of going to live on a Greek island. Another wants a ranch in Montana or Wyoming. "I have a recurring daydream," she confides, "about getting up in the morning, saddling up my horse, and riding out to see where my cattle are." Unlike people in other occupations who harbor such fantasies, these women are in a position to make their dreams real. At $300,000—or $500,000 or $1 million—a year, the phrase "early retirement" takes on a whole new meaning. It isn't unheard-of for Wall Streeters, male or female, to retire in their mid-thirties and live comfortably ever after.

IF WOMEN'S EGOS are not directly linked to their bank balances, it's doubtless due to decades of conditioning. Susan Byrne, the champion stock picker who founded and runs Westwood Management, admits to a powerful ambivalence about her own success. "Women like me, who were raised with very traditional middle-class values and expectations, have *tremendous* cultural stigmas and fears to overcome," she says. "There is a very deep-rooted feeling, particularly in women over thirty-five, that it's unfeminine to be able to take care of yourself financially, that it makes you less lovable. Somehow, unconsciously, women are afraid that if they're competent with money they'll end up alone."

Susan has noticed the same mindset in so many other prosperous women that she has dubbed it the Mildred Pierce Syndrome—no less a malady than Trader Head, but with diametrically opposite symptoms. Mildred Pierce was the heroine of the eponymous 1945 Joan Crawford film—a strong, capable, and rather offputtingly frosty woman who runs a successful restaurant business, and whose iron-spined ambition drives her husband away. The movie is a classic of its kind, the World War II–era morality tale, and Crawford won an Oscar for her part in it.

The message *Mildred Pierce* conveyed couldn't be clearer: any woman not delighted to stay home, blithely and trustfully letting her husband arrange her financial well-being, must be a heartless, castrating bitch. It's a stereotypical view of half of humankind, as black-and-white as the frames that flashed onto the silver screen. But it impressed its audience profoundly, and it lingers. And lingers. And keeps on scaring women who might otherwise have more sense and more self-knowledge than to believe it.

Susan claims to suffer vestigial traces of the Mildred Pierce Syndrome herself. "I still feel a certain amount of resistance to being financially competent," she admits. "For instance, I'll be trying to figure out the best interest rate on a co-op apartment I want to buy as an investment, and my mind will just go *blank*. If I were doing the same calculations for someone else, a friend, say, or certainly a client, I'd have no problem. I'd be razor sharp. But when it's *my own* money, it's the Mildred Pierce Syndrome again."

It's easy for an outside observer to pooh-pooh this problem by pointing out that, hey, it isn't 1945 anymore, so get over it, already. But alas, life at the top of the income heap is not so simple. To hear Wall Street women tell it, most men they meet today still think and act like Mildred Pierce's cringing husband. It's a phenomenon as common as taxes, and more nettlesome. Men frequently claim to be attracted to smart, financially independent women. Yet, wrestling with some awkward cultural baggage of their own, they also find such women, well, *scary.*

Nearly every woman on Wall Street has at least one discouraging tale, and usually several, to tell. "Men you meet socially do resent you for making money and getting ahead," says a female investment banker whose net worth long ago sailed past the million-dollar mark and keeps right on climbing. "I think they're afraid they can't measure up. It's as if they want half of you, just half. They can't handle *all* of you. You're too much."

Pat Jehle, the Salomon whiz kid who invented securities backed by credit-card and car loans, tells of dating a Frenchman who was quickly daunted by her demanding job, her plush East Side apartment, her summer beach house, her sports car. "You live," he told her by way of farewell, "like a man." Says Pat: "It gets to where having a lot of money that you earned yourself starts to seem like having a mustache or a tattoo. No matter how 'feminine' you are in every other way, you still aren't quite perceived as a 'real woman.'"

Some women have seen so many romances wrecked by the money issue that they've taken to lying about their jobs. One investment banker, flourishing at a prosperous old-line firm, relates a typical instance: "Once a friend wanted to fix me up with a nice single guy she knew, and she had already mentioned to him where I work, but not what I do. So we went out to dinner, and I could tell he was kind of insecure about his own career. So, when he finally got around to asking me what I did, I told him I was a secretary." She laughs ruefully. "Well, he didn't believe me. So then I told him the truth, although I really made light of it—you know, like, just a job, no big deal. We saw each other a couple of times after that, but later I heard he was engaged to a woman who really *was* a secretary." She shrugs. "They're married now." The investment banker is still single, and not happy about it.

Elaine Garzarelli, the Shearson market strategist who accurately predicted Black Monday, remembers a similar experience. During the years she spent developing her forecasting method, she dated a man who encouraged her and urged her on. But, once she had arrived at the top of her profession, he backed away: "I think the problem was that *his* career wasn't going the way he wanted it to, so when I started being on television and so on, it bothered him. After we broke up, he married a schoolteacher."

Partly because many men tend to see money as symbolic of power, they cling to some moldy old ideas about chivalry, wherein the knight on the white horse—or in the white Lamborghini— saves the fair damsel in distress. A woman who happens to have earned a few million dollars is not, by these men's lights, in need of rescue. Says longtime portfolio manager Suzanne Jaffe, a little wistfully, "Oh, they *admire* you, they *like* you. But they think you don't need them."

After the defection of the man who married the schoolteacher, Elaine Garzarelli began seeing an attorney who, being quite wealthy himself, was less intimidated by her salary. "Still," she recalls, "he would do things around my apartment. Like, he'd come over and want to change the light bulbs. Once I put in a new rheostat switch, you know, a dimmer switch. I hooked up the wires all by myself, which is really not that hard to do. But it bugged him that I did that. Whether it's money or some other thing, like being handy around the house, men don't feel comfortable if you're too independent." She smiles, a shy, private smile, and adds softly, "Well, I mean, they need to be *needed.* But everyone does. Everyone wants to be loved, don't they?"

Indeed. Even Wall Street women.

In the effort to stave off permanent singlehood, female financiers often adopt one of two strategies, both of which involve bypassing the vast majority of middle-class men altogether. Stated as a general rule, they boil down to this: either find a man who makes even more money than you do, so he won't feel threatened by yours, or find a man whose criteria for success have little to do with money at all, so that he doesn't know how much you've got and, even better, doesn't care. In practical terms, then, most Wall Street women pair off with fellow finance mavens of an equal or higher rank, or with artists—painters, musicians, playwrights, actors. Fortunately, there is no shortage of any of those in New York; but the search for a soulmate takes some extra patience and perseverance, in these circumstances, and gives single Wall Street women a surfeit of solitary evenings to spend reflecting on what money can't buy.

THE IRRATIONAL but persistent whiff of social stigma that attaches to self-made women naturally exerts a moderating influence on what they do with all that cash. One might, for instance, imagine them awash in jewels, furs, and designer-original clothes. One would be wrong. Granted, some do confess to a weakness for shopping. Elaine Garzarelli, for instance, loves to buy clothes—"especially when the market is up. It's a way of celebrating." But, on the principle that if you've got it you'd better not flaunt it, most Wall Street women dress no differently than, say, the average female executive in publishing, advertising, or insurance.

Indeed, many seem to go out of their way to dress down. Take the matter of fur coats. One of the many peculiarities of life in New York is that so many people, including clerk-typists, unemployed actresses, and even journalists, own at least one fur. This is largely because, hereabouts, a fur is both cheaper and more practical than a car. With all the walking that New Yorkers do, and in weather that makes the phrase "Moscow on the Hudson" seem like more than just the name of a movie, warmth may outrank glamour as a reason for the purchase. And the environs of Wall Street, hard by New York harbor with its arctic whistling winds, are surely Manhattan Island's chilliest. Yet trading-floor coatrooms and office coatracks at firms like Salomon Brothers, Merrill Lynch, and First Boston are conspicuously short of minks and sables. As Richard Nixon once boasted of his wife, Pat, the average Wall Street woman wears "a good Republican cloth coat."

Likewise, if she drives at all—and many don't—a female investment banker or trader is far more likely to own a Jeep or a Saab than a Ferrari or a Porsche. Davia Temin, the marketing chief at Scudder, Stevens & Clark, goes chugging out to the Hamptons every summer in an ancient Volvo. Laurie Hawkes at Salomon Brothers drives a Ford. Chase's Leslie Daniels owns a beat-up old Toyota. "It's partly, I think, that we aren't trying to *prove* anything by our possessions," Leslie reflects. "A lot of men tend to get ego gratification by way of conspicuous consumption. We don't seem to need to do that."

So what *do* they spend their money on? The answers are strikingly varied, and often quite original. For Laurie Hawkes, the best part of being prosperous is sending her parents, siblings, and in-laws on fully paid vacations in Europe, Australia, and other far-flung pleasure spots. "I like playing fairy godmother," she says. When they can spare the time, which isn't often, female financiers take some pretty lavish vacations themselves—where, perhaps not coincidentally, self-indulgent spending can occur well out of sight of friends, lovers, and colleagues. Brenda Landry, the Morgan Stanley research analyst, relishes the memory of the time she and her husband chartered a luxury yacht for a leisurely winter cruise through the Galápagos Islands. The trip included some close encounters with the famous giant sea turtles there—"They like to have their throats stroked," Brenda says—and a sighting, via high-powered telescope, of Halley's Comet. Ginnie Clark is a regular on the posh ski slopes of Colorado and Vermont, where an icy wind whooshing in her ears on a downhill run drowns out the clamorous echoes of the trading floor.

But lack of time, combined with down-to-earth attitudes about money, most often inclines Wall Street women toward hobbies that double as solid investments. One of these is art collections. Davia

Temin, an art-history buff since college days, lives in an apartment on the nineteenth floor of a luxury high-rise overlooking the shining sweep of the East River. The place is decorated with a selection of Ukiyo-e prints from seventeenth-century Japan. "Ukiyo-e" means "floating worlds," a reference to Tokyo's so-called water trade, the shimmering night life that revolves around tea houses and public baths. The Ukiyo-e printmakers were the first Japanese artists to depict scenes of ordinary people enjoying everyday pleasures—a sharp break from a centuries-long tradition of art devoted exclusively to royal and religious scenes and figures. Ukiyo-e was a movement that greatly influenced the Impressionists, especially the painter Degas, in nineteenth-century Europe.

Davia owns about 135 Ukiyo-e prints. One of them is pictured in a book, *The Great Wave,* published by the Metropolitan Museum of Art, which describes the effects of Japanese prints on the French artistic imagination. In this work, which hangs above Davia's dining table, a snow-covered bridge arches over a blue stream meandering into the distance. Two figures in kimonos, their backs to the viewer and heads bowed in conversation, cross the bridge. A third has already reached the far shore. In her living room, curled up on a green velvet sofa with a portfolio of other unframed prints open on her lap, Davia looks fondly at a framed specimen on the opposite wall, wherein a black cat crouches, staring out an open window at a distant volcano. "It draws you in, doesn't it?" she says. "The serenity of looking at the looker. And a certain air of mystery.

"Now, *this* one—" she turns and points to another, on the wall behind her—"this is one of my very favorites." White foxes stand on a hillside against a night-blue background. They hold yellow-burning flames in their narrow jaws, and the flames are reflected in the stars in the sky. According to Japanese legend, foxes holding fire are a sign of a coming catastrophe, a portentous event. Such as, perhaps, October 19, 1987.

A less esoteric investment with great appeal to Wall Street

women is that old standby, real estate. Many hold properties worth millions. Elaine Garzarelli, for instance, owns not just one but two co-op apartments in the same Manhattan luxury building: she lives in one, and keeps the other ready for relatives and clients who visit from out of town. She also has the obligatory beach house in the Hamptons for the odd weekend when she can get away from work. Brenda Landry buys properties and boosts their value with extensive renovations. "Apart from work, my main passion is real estate," she declares. "I *love* to fix up houses." She and her stockbroker husband own a townhouse on Manhattan's Upper East Side, a summer house on Long Island, and a third place in Sarasota, Florida. That Sarasota house has been time-consuming: "I am *constantly* on the phone with contractors, electricians, designers.... There's nothing *left* of the original house, except the roof. And the kitchen sink."

The process is no doubt less enervating from a distance. Laurie Hawkes and her husband, a venture capitalist, bought an imposing six-bedroom Tudor manse in Bronxville, New York—an affluent enclave about a half-hour by commuter train from Grand Central Station—and lived in it while they renovated. "There have been times I thought we must be crazy," Laurie says with a sigh. "At one point we had thirteen different people working on the house— spackling, painting, papering, putting in three entire new bathrooms, knocking out the wall that divided the servants' quarters from the rest of the house. You just wouldn't have believed it. Two years of dust, noise, and chaos." Sitting in her spacious living room, with its shining hardwood floors and wall of leaded windowpanes, Laurie looks out on a peaceful leafy street under a spring twilight the color of a pearl. She adds with a contented grin: "But now that it's done, I think it's all been worth it."

Inspired by the success of that project, Laurie and her husband started a little business on the side. They bought a historic mansion in Greenwich, Connecticut, with the idea of restoring it and reselling it at a profit. "We did this because I thought it would be a fun hobby," Laurie says. "Little did I know!" Their timing was unfortunate. In October of 1987, while Laurie's employer undertook well-publicized mass layoffs and the stock market hit the skids, Laurie and Paul were trying to get bank financing for their real-estate enterprise, which they dubbed LHTW Corp. The initials stood for "Let's Hope This Works," although, Laurie notes, "We didn't tell the bankers that."

Potential lenders were nervous enough already. And, since they had put a big chunk of their own savings into the venture and needed banks' help to finish the renovation, so were Laurie and Paul. "I was the only person in America with *no* stocks in my personal portfolio who panicked that October anyway," Laurie recalls. "I went through several stomach linings. And my husband would wake me up at night and say, 'How can you *sleep?* We could be *ruined.*'" She bought him some cocktail napkins that read "MONEY ISN'T EVERYTHING, but it quiets my nerves."

At last, after several tense weeks, Citicorp agreed to help finance the rest of the project, which went ahead without a hitch from then on. In May of 1988, LHTW Corp. put Berkeley Manor on the market, with its manicured two-and-a-half-acre grounds, circular driveway, newly refurbished swimming pool, eight bedrooms, et cetera, et cetera. The asking price of $3.6 million—which would have been a bargain by upper-crust Connecticut standards, in the free-spending days of the bull market—proved in the new post-Crash real estate lull to be a bit steep. As of mid-1989, Berkeley Manor was still for sale. The house earned its keep by appearing as a backdrop in photographs for tony catalogues, and in August stood a good chance of serving as a set for a movie starring Glenn Close and Jeremy Irons. "We'd still like to sell it, though," Laurie said. "We'd consider taking $3.35 million."

SUCH VISIBLE ASSETS notwithstanding, a remarkably high proportion of female financiers' wealth is salted away in familiar, and generally quite conservative, securities: blue-chip stocks (with a preponderance of preferred shares, not common, thank you), convertible bonds, bank certificates of deposit. One investment banker in her early thirties—who asked to remain anonymous, perhaps in case any future dates are reading this—confesses that in each year since 1981 she has invested more than half of her seven-figure income this way. "I know it sounds like a cliché, but I work hard and I want my money to work hard too," she says. "I don't fritter it away on anything frivolous. And I don't like unnecessary risk."

Speaking for many successful women on the Street, she points out that being female, especially if one is also single, does have certain clear advantages in this regard. "I'm lucky that I *can* put aside so much of my income for investments. A lot of my colleagues are guys in their mid-forties. They've got a wife up in Darien [Connecticut] or on Park Avenue, with a maid and a country-club membership, two kids at Yale and Princeton and a third at Choate, a couple of big mortgages. They *have* to shell out a lot of money, don't they?

"I don't have those obligations. Who am I going to spend money on? My cat? So I invest it instead. And just watch it grow." Thanks to some shrewd moves during the bull market, and a few lucky decisions just before the Crash, this investment banker estimates her fortune, as of mid-1988, at about $14 million. Now, she cheerfully admits, "I'm working mostly for the fun of it."

Remember Aesop's fable of the grasshopper and the ant? In the story, which like all fables used to be taught to children as a cautionary tale, the grasshopper spent the summer playing and lounging in the sun. He wondered, and scoffed a bit, at the strange behavior of the ant, who toiled busily at storing crumbs of food for the coming winter. The fable's ending is both predictable and grim. When the cold weather came, the grasshopper panicked and perished. The wise and rather irritatingly self-righteous ant, of course, ate well and prospered.

Once arrogance had given way to anxiety all up and down Wall Street and in financial markets around the world, the flashy young male hotshots of yesteryear came to resemble so many feckless grasshoppers. Guess who the ants were. Whether goaded by the fear of seeming "unfeminine"; inspired by the yearning for long-term security; freed by the absence of costly family commitments; or motivated by commonsensical caution, most female financiers have piled up fewer debts and expenses, and stashed away more savings and investments, than many of their male counterparts.

They are, mercifully, a lot less smug about it than the ant in the fable. "I think it's just that women are more pessimistic by nature. We seem to be more aware that everything is transitory, even a wild bull market. We're always waiting for the pendulum to swing the other way and hit us in the head," says topnotch Merrill Lynch stockbroker Judy Connolly.

A paragon of frugality, Judy still lives in the same modest apartment where she lived ten years ago, when she started at Merrill Lynch—except that, in those days, she was a secretary, earning about one-tenth her current annual pay. Still, her idea of wanton extravagance, even now, is to spring for a couple of $50 theater tickets once a week or so.

"I like the security of knowing I could always go back to typing, if I had to, and never have to starve doing it," she explains. "Rather than run out and buy a Porsche or a palace, I'd rather have that peace of mind." Wall Street women have discovered that, whatever the momentary state of markets in these mercurial times, peace of mind—unlike a Porsche, a *palazzo,* or a Piper Cub—is priceless.

In the year that followed Black Monday, uneasiness about big-time greed was increasingly pervasive. Indeed, 1988 may turn out to be remembered, in the long run, as the year when pessimism became fashionable. Some mergers-and-acquisitions specialists, especially those doing lucrative but controversial leveraged buyouts, remained exuberant. They apparently took to heart economist

John Maynard Keynes's famously carefree remark, "In the long run, we're all dead." So enjoy, enjoy. But other Wall Street denizens, even some of those most enriched by the corporate-takeover boom, began to decry its possible effects.

Consider Martin Lipton. A partner in the distinguished law firm of Wachtell Lipton Rosen & Katz, he reportedly had been paid the fattest legal fee in history — $20 million, or more than $5,000 an hour — for his work on the $13.4 billion Philip Morris acquisition of Kraft Inc. Nevertheless, in late October of 1988, Lipton wrote a scarifying two-page memo to his firm's clients. It said, in part, that "our nation is blindly rushing to the precipice ... [and] we and our children will pay a gigantic price for allowing abusive takeover tactics and bootstrap, junk-bond takeovers." The ultimate result of these megadeals, Lipton predicted, would be another stock-market crash.

The reason for such worry, which had spread to Congress and spawned a batch of special committees, was not far to seek. Largely thanks to mergers, acquisitions, and leveraged buyouts they had accomplished with boggling amounts of borrowed money, American corporations staggered under an unprecedented load of debt. In 1980, according to the U.S. Federal Reserve Board, companies' debts, though hardly small beer, were still equal to only about 81 percent of their assets. By the end of 1988, debt exceeded assets — stood, to be precise, at 104 percent of assets — so that corporate America's net worth was underwater by 4 percentage points.

Linda Costello, a senior vice president at Dean Witter, who had helped to put together dozens of leveraged buyouts, observed over lunch in late November of 1988: "Even people who have been doing these deals for years — whom you might expect to be interested only in the fees — are starting to get a little queasy about these pointless multi-billion-dollar maneuvers. The RJR Nabisco deal, at $25 billion, struck a lot of people as just outrageous. Suddenly you get a strong feeling, talking to other investment bankers, that some sort of limit has been reached, and common sense is beginning to intrude." Apparently as a consequence, the number of mergers and acquisitions fell off sharply in the early months of 1989, the first such decline in years. A few huge deals, like the vitriolic three-way takeover fight of Time Inc., Warner Communications, and Paramount, continued to make headlines. But, as Paul K. Kelly, president of the merchant bank Peers & Co. observed: "Although debt is neither morally correct nor incorrect, it has taken on a negative connotation." Nervous investors stayed out of a $1.5 billion leveraged-buyout fund established by Shearson Lehman Hutton. Morgan Stanley and Goldman, Sachs, formerly gung-ho, got leery of taking on huge hostile acquisitions; and Salomon Brothers began to back away from the business of making bridge loans to clients who had big, overly risky (or just plain silly) deals in mind, and in the first half of 1989 all but disappeared from the junk-bond business.

The undertone of unease will probably shape Wall Street's mood, and much of its business, well into the nineties. If so, then female financiers, with their habit of keeping a low financial profile and their relatively risk-averse leanings, will once again have been only a little bit ahead of their time.

III.

WHERE THEY

CAME FROM

I f the bull market made Wall Street seem from afar like the glittering Emerald City of Oz, the post-Crash doldrums have endowed it with all the glamour of Kansas. Students at the top graduate business schools, many of whom set out to pursue an M.B.A. because it was the ticket to investment banking, began having second thoughts. A Harvard student survey revealed, for instance, that only 11 percent of the 1988 M.B.A. class hoped to head for Wall Street—down from 30 percent in 1987, and more than 50 percent the year before that. At Stanford, five M.B.A. students were offered Wall Street jobs in the first three months of 1988; four turned them down. The reason, explained Elizabeth Meyer, director of the school's career-management center, was that "something else like October 19 [1987] could happen."

The cooling of enthusiasm for careers on the Street arose, of course, from uncertainty about the future direction of the markets, and, like that uncertainty, marked a settling back to the *status quo ante*. Hard as it was to keep in mind in the eighties, when newly minted M.B.A.s were jostling each other for jobs at even the least prestigious firms, Wall Street has not always held much appeal for people fresh out of school. Indeed, some who ended up thriving in the business say they had to overcome an aversion to the place before they could bring themselves to work on the Street at all.

For women, who until the early eighties were made to feel thoroughly unwelcome in the boys'-club culture of big securities firms, misgivings were understandable, and sometimes quite strong. Laurie Hawkes, for one, recalls that the idea of working at Salomon Brothers initially inspired a reluctance that bordered on revulsion. Her first encounter with an investment-banking recruiter convinced her, she says, that Wall Street "must be the most *awful* place on *earth.*" As a graduate student at Cornell in 1978, she went to a career-planning seminar, where she met the first Wall Streeter she'd ever laid eyes on: "The recruiter from Salomon was outrageous. He was a hard-talking guy, you know, one of these macho types: 'We eat women and children for breakfast' kind of attitude. 'We separate the men from the boys.' " She laughs. "I was disgusted."

Nothing in Laurie's experience had prepared her for Salomon's particular style of tougher-than-thou posturing. She grew up in a small New England town and went to Bowdoin College in Brunswick, Maine. There she majored in biochemistry: "I was hell-bent on medical school."

Toward that end, she spent her junior year as an exchange student at the University of Nairobi in Kenya. Her keenest memory of the university is a startling legacy of violent student uprisings during Kenya's emergence from British rule in the sixties. Wide beds of flowers encircled the campus, vivid with a sprawling profusion of white, pink, and orange blossoms, as delicate as morning glories. Spectacular from a distance—but the vines and blooms concealed expanses of high-voltage electrified barbed wire, laid flat on the ground beneath. With the flick of a switch, those pretty flower beds could become a weapon, or a barricade.

As part of her premed training, Laurie worked in a clinic and a maternity hospital. "I was the only white person working in the clinic. People would stand in the doorway and stare at me. Little giggling kids would run up and touch my skin," she remembers, chuckling. "I didn't learn much Swahili, except the words for 'Three teaspoons a day, one in the morning, one at noon, one in the evening.' It was hard to get people to listen, though. You would give the patient a bottle of medicine, and he would stand outside in the parking lot and chug it. The other thing I was supposed to do was teach birth control. It wasn't easy because, in that culture, people measure their wealth by how many children they have. So you can imagine they were very skeptical of what I was telling them. Polite, but 'No thanks, lady.' " She grins. "I delivered six babies."

That year, Laurie also joined an expedition that climbed Mount Kilimanjaro. "I was thinking about Hemingway. You know, 'The Snows of Kilimanjaro'?" At about seventeen thousand feet, literary musings went by the wayside: Laurie got such a wretched case of altitude sickness that the guides urged her to turn back.

She refused, and she's not sorry. On the last leg of the ascent, the part she would have missed, the climbers reached a vast bowl of rocks, whitish, nearly colorless. "It looked like the surface of the moon," she recalls. "When we got there, it started to snow hard. We hiked across that lunar landscape in a blizzard. It was *unreal.* Just unreal." Laurie spent the night high on the mountain, along with one other woman she had talked into staying with her; the rest of the group headed back to a camp station partway down. "In the morning we took pictures of the sunrise. Unbelievable, like the dawn of Creation," she says. "It was fantastic."

At other times, Laurie and a few fellow students hitchhiked or took buses all over Kenya and Tanzania. It was a fourteen-hour ride to Dar es Salaam, crammed into a rickety old bus on hard wooden seats. Once they got there, she and her companions were promptly robbed. Laurie got stranded on the way to Zanzibar; went fishing in the Indian Ocean; stood *this close* to giraffes, elephants, zebras on the African plains. "I can't stand to see animals in cages," she says now. "Zoos make me queasy." More than anything else, she was fascinated by the people she met: "College kids in Nairobi were so much more politically aware than the kids I knew back in Maine. They challenged my comfortable middle-class American assumptions about everything, what's right, what's fair, politics, life. They made me *think*."

It was in Kenya that Laurie abandoned the idea of medical school. The government's Ministry of Health had hired the international consulting firm of Booz, Allen & Hamilton to think up efficient ways of getting medical care to people living in remote reaches of the country. Laurie did some of the research for Booz, Allen's study, and liked the work so much that she decided to go into international health-care consulting. "To do that, I needed a business degree. So after I finished at Bowdoin I went to Cornell. Then after a year at Cornell I ran out of money."

Her college boyfriend, Paul, who is now her husband, was living in Boston at the time, so she went there. "By sheer luck, Wellesley Hospital was looking for an intern in administration to set up a day-care center and do some financial analysis and planning," she says. "That was the job that piqued my interest in finance." After nine months, she went back to Cornell—and ran straight into that macho Salomon recruiter.

She tells what happened next with an impish spark in her dark-blue eyes: "So. I did not want to work on the Street *at all.* I knew nothing about it and cared even less, but this man from Salomon wanted to interview me, and Paul told me to go and see. I was the only person being interviewed who wasn't dying to make an impression. I had a background in *health care,* for heaven's sake, and the interviewers and I were about equally surprised that I showed up." She laughs. "And you should have *seen* me. I had just gotten this bargain Afro haircut, it was supposed to be a perm but it looked awful, and I was wearing shoes I'd borrowed from my roommate. I felt really awkward because I looked so frumpy, and then I walked into the office at Cornell where the Salomon people were doing their thing and there was that *same obnoxious guy* from the seminar." She lets out a hoot of laughter. "I almost got up and ran out."

She stayed for a highly unorthodox encounter. First Laurie asked the man from Salomon point-blank why he wanted to interview her. His answer, as she remembers it: "Well, once in a while we like to get a mixed bag. We like to talk to different kinds of people." When they had squared off for half an hour or so, he offered her a summer job at the firm. "My last summer job, the year before, was in a women's prison in Maine," she says. "So I told him, 'I know very little about your business.'" His answer: "No, that's wrong. You know *nothing* about our business. But I think you can learn it." He then asked Laurie to come out for a beer, and the two of them, and one other Salomon interviewer, piled into Laurie's battered Volkswagen bug and went to a local dive and had a very fine time.

The "obnoxious guy," Peter Feldman, turned out to be a valued friend and mentor once Laurie got to Salomon. "He hired some of the best people here, including my boss," says Laurie fondly. That first summer, Feldman also rented Laurie an apartment he owned in Manhattan's opulent and pricey Sutton Place. "To give you an idea of how well I knew New York, when he offered it to me I asked him, 'Sutton Place? Is that a nice neighborhood?' *Ha.* The *look* he gave me: 'What a hick this kid is.'"

LAURIE IS HARDLY alone in having turned up her nose, at first, at the idea of a career in finance. Most other Wall Street women also set out to do something entirely unrelated, and arrived on the Street by circuitous—not to say haphazard—routes. Few cared about business as undergraduates. Patricia Douglas, the commercial-paper whiz at Shearson Lehman Hutton, majored in English literature in college. "People often ask me, 'Did you always want to do this kind of work?' " she says with a laugh. "I don't know if they think I was reading the *Wall Street Journal* when I was ten or what. I didn't even know what this *was* until after I got here."

Jessica Palmer, a managing director in the capital-markets group at Salomon Brothers, had even less of a clue early on: British by birth, she grew up on a coffee plantation in Kenya. Her parents still live there, and her mother, Ann Palmer, turns up now and then in films that are shot on location nearby. In the Oscar-winning 1985 movie *Out of Africa,* Jessica's mum played the classy blond dowager who fired the pistol and shouted "God save the Queen!" on the stroke of midnight at the New Year's Eve party where, moviegoers may recall, Robert Redford finally got around to kissing Meryl Streep.

Jessica began her career working for Wells Fargo, the San Francisco–based commercial bank, in London in the buttoned-down mid-seventies. "It's funny, the way life is," she says now, "and how easily you could have ended up doing something completely different. When I was working in London, it was clear that financial houses were literally run by the secretaries, who of course were all women, and who got no credit for it and were paid a pittance. If Wells Fargo hadn't sent me to San Francisco when they did, I might have stayed there in London and started a secretaries' union." She adds with a devilish grin, "I might have had quite a career as a trade unionist."

Louis Rukeyser once introduced Shearson's Elaine Garzarelli on the TV show *Wall Street Week* by saying: "It's not known whether any mother ever bounced a baby on her knee and said, 'I sure hope she will grow up to be a quantitative market strategist.' But, in any event, that's what happened to Elaine Garzarelli." It could easily have happened otherwise. Although by now she seems perfectly in her element on Wall Street, a natural, her aspiration when she was growing up in the Philadelphia suburb of Springfield was to be a chemist. "I used to sit in my room and do chemistry experiments and watch *American Bandstand,*" she recalls. "Besides my chemistry set, what I loved was dancing. I lived for dances, although I wasn't allowed to go on real dates very much. My family is Italian and very old-world conservative, very strict. When we were small, my mother pushed us pretty hard. We couldn't just go out and play like other kids, we had all kinds of lessons instead—elocution lessons, dance lessons, music lessons. . . . She even taught us how to type.

"My brother was the kid who got all A's, all the time. So I felt like the black sheep, the dumb one in the family." When Elaine went to college, her father, a banker, urged her to major in business; she studied chemical engineering instead. Then she took a required economics course in her junior year, and decided as a consequence to change her major—not because she thought it would pay better, as it indisputably has, but because she found economic formulas more fun than the chemical kind.

In the not-so-distant days of the mid- to late seventies, and for decades before that, it was possible—even common—to do quite well for oneself on the Street without first taking a single graduate business course. Lots of high-powered men, in fact, scrapped their way from lowly spots as runners on the floor of the New York Stock Exchange all the way up to the executive committees of their firms, without ever having set foot on a college campus at all. Women who chose the same path, counting on hard work and a native knack for numbers to make up for relatively humble academic credentials, are sometimes proud of it. Ellen Lee, the almost defiantly "feminine" managing director of Ernst & Co., has never hidden her lack of an M.B.A. "I got to Wall Street," she likes to say, "by taking the commuter train from New Jersey." Ask her if she has a master's degree and she answers, "No, thank God."

She hasn't really needed one. Her first job after graduating from Seton Hall University in 1973 was at Prudential-Bache, the brokerage house then known as Bache Halsey Stuart Shields. When Bache promoted her to assistant vice president in 1977, the firm also made her a floor trader, buying and selling thousands of shares of stock every day on behalf of Bache brokers and their customers. At age twenty-five, she was the first woman to represent a major brokerage firm on the floor of the New York Stock Exchange.

The distinction got her picture wired everywhere by United Press International and printed on the "people" pages of newspapers and magazines around the country, alongside the likes of Robert Redford and John Travolta. But it didn't endear her to colleagues, who regarded her as young, brash, and underqualified. "A lot of my peers, especially men, resented me," she concedes with a shrug. "There were questions about what my father did and who I was sleeping with." Her father is the manager of a Shop-Rite supermarket in New Jersey, which means, Ellen notes, that "as far as influence on the Street is concerned, he might as well be on Mars."

Of course, before Wall Street enjoyed its brief, shining half-decade as the hottest place in America to go looking for a job, plenty of men, too, had other career plans in college, didn't get master's degrees, and arrived on the Street almost by chance. But for women there was another, distinctly "feminine" force prevailing. As girls growing up in the fifties and early sixties, many never expected to have careers at all, and most who did were steered by parents and teachers toward the so-called "helping professions"—teaching, social work, nursing, secretarial work—or the arts.

Some spent years there. It's unheard-of to find a man in high finance who used to be a grade-school teacher or a welfare caseworker. Plenty of women on Wall Street, though, have such entries on their résumés. "Women have such diverse backgrounds because we *are* women—especially but not only those of us over thirty-five," says Goldman, Sachs municipal-finance innovator Ann Kaplan. She holds a master's degree in social work from Columbia. "When we were in college, nobody told us we could go into investment banking. Most of us really thought business was just for men. So we gravitated at first toward 'women's work.'"

It's a familiar tune, but what is surprising is how deftly women have used their previous, ostensibly unrelated job experience, applying it to Wall Street in unexpected ways, and finding subtle but essential connections. It would be hard to imagine a more striking exemplar of this phenomenon than Merrill Lynch's first female trader, Ginnie Clark. In 1964, fresh out of Oklahoma State University—where she earned a degree in psychology and won a slew of beauty contests—Ginnie wasn't sure what to do next. So she took a summer job in Las Vegas, dealing twenty-one on the night shift from 10 p.m. to 6 a.m., in Harrah's casino.

Apart from handling the cards, her main function was to charm the gamblers with her big beauty-queen smile. What they had no way of knowing was that the beaming blonde behind the counter regarded their losses with incomprehension: Ginnie had beaten the system the very first time she played the game. She knew which cards were coming next. It was easy—just a series of numbers, instantly memorized, the missing ones mentally filled in. All it took was a fantastic memory and a sure feel for the probabilities. For a Wall Street trader, of course, these talents—unteachable in any business school—are like a license to print money.

Joanne Tillemans, the Salomon Brothers trainee who went off to London to sell bonds, might seem at first blush to have been an even unlikelier financier. Born in Wisconsin, Joanne spent most of her childhood in Breckenridge, Minnesota, a wide spot in the road on the North Dakota border, where the tallest building for miles around was the local grain elevator. When she left home at the age of seventeen, it wasn't to go to college, much less to business school: it was to see the world and become a professional dancer.

First, Joanne moved around the country for a while—Vermont, California, Minneapolis, Mexico, back to Minneapolis. Alighting in the Twin Cities for a second time, Joanne joined a dance company and found, she thought, her true vocation: "I *loved* it. I was always flat broke but that didn't seem like a burden because I was so *into* it." And she was good at it. By age twenty-three, she had more than two hundred professional performances under her belt, and a federal arts-in-the-schools grant that paid her $15 an hour to "teach teachers in public schools how to teach kids to dance."

At that moment in the mid-seventies, Minneapolis—a gem of a small city, with its clean, friendly downtown and meandering string of green riverside parks—was just becoming what it still is: a major Midwestern magnet for serious artists of all kinds who have reason to be dissatisfied with both coasts. Dance in particular was hot; so when Joanne, at twenty-four, started her own dance company, it quickly caught fire. Called Contactworks, the company attracted the attention and collaboration of the New York elite. "Oh, we did workshops with Twyla Tharp. And Andrew DeGroat. And John Case." Joanne's cornflower-blue eyes go a little vague. She sighs. "And Meredith Monk." Pause. "It was a great feeling of . . . *building* something."

It was the hope of a big-time dance career that brought Joanne to New York. But living in New York in bohemian poverty, as anyone who's tried it can tell you, is not so thrilling. "I almost went home to Minnesota a thousand times," says Joanne. "I got a big loft in Soho that I rented out as a performance space. I had Russian balalaika orchestras practicing there, and avant-garde performance artists bouncing off the walls—no privacy at all. And these enormous rats. When I first heard them I thought somebody was breaking in." After a couple of months, Joanne got a job waiting tables at The Bottom Line, a jazz club in Greenwich Village. And she danced. While her performances got encouraging write-ups in the *Village Voice* and the *New York Times,* she was more and more unhappy.

"So one day I took a long walk and I thought, 'Is this worth it?' Everybody I knew, all the dancers who were older than I was, were still so poor, and they would have these crushing bouts of depression. And anyway I was tired of artists. I was sick of listening to people who would spend an entire afternoon talking about a twinge in one elbow or a slight stiffness in one knee. And, believe me, that is what dancers talk about."

Joanne breaks off and sips coffee for a minute, far away in thought, staring out the window at the Statue of Liberty in the harbor below. Then she says, "You know, people on Wall Street are more open-minded than artists are. Artists *think* they are very open-minded, but they live in a very closed community, mostly below Fourteenth Street. It's hard to do anything, as an artist, that reaches anybody outside that little closed circle."

As her first tentative step outside the circle, Joanne enrolled in night school at Hunter College in Manhattan, majoring in economics with a minor in math: "By that time I had moved again. I was living in a terrible dumpy apartment on the Lower East Side. I did a lot of studying on the subways. My escape was math problems. I would spend hours and hours doing math problems." It turned out to be a felicitous use of time. Joanne's grade-point average at Hunter was a flawless 4.0. And that impressed admissions officers at Stanford, where Joanne gratefully fled to pursue her M.B.A. under the kind California sun. "I was euphoric," she says now.

Even so, after a couple of years, New York exerted a powerful pull. "I wanted to come back," she says. "I just didn't want to come back broke. I had always been so poor here before. You know, you always have a personal relationship with this city, or any city, and I had always been on the wrong side of it, cramming for exams on the subways, staring out my window at an airshaft. I wanted to see what it would be like to live here with money." Wall Street could certainly offer that. So, when Salomon Brothers' recruiters came calling in the spring of 1985, Joanne was intrigued. "It seemed like a perfect career move," she says, "because I figured no matter *what* I decided to do later, working for an investment bank would be fantastic, as a way of balancing out all that arts experience on my résumé."

Initially, all those years of dancing made Salomon skeptical. In

San Francisco, Joanne met with a recruiter from the firm named Ken Matthews. She recalls the encounter with a sheepish little giggle: "I spent an hour talking and talking, telling him why I thought I belonged on Wall Street. He didn't say a word. Just stared out the window the whole time. It was *maddening.*

"Finally I said that being a dancer was like being an athlete. You need the same kind of energy level, and flexibility, and concentration. And you have the same kinds of ups and downs—one day you're really 'on,' one day you're not. I thought working on the trading floor, either trading or selling, would be similar. He looked at me and said, 'That's good. Remember that.' "

The three-way analogy won over her subsequent interviewers, and it still strikes her as valid: dance is similar in many ways to sport, and both are much like bond trading. "The trading floor is almost a theatrical arena. In fact, not even 'almost': it's the most dramatic theater I've ever seen. You are always at center stage. Everything you do is visible. And you cannot afford, *ever,* to let your emotions control you. It's just like performing."

A background in "women's work" can come in especially handy in selling or marketing jobs on the Street. Although Judy Connolly is a broker now, she used to be a schoolteacher, and much of the time she feels she's still teaching. "Most of my clients aren't jet-set types," she explains. "They are just nice middle-class people who have accumulated a lot of money somehow or other. It's helpful sometimes to have been a teacher, because you can explain things that are pretty complicated in terms your clients can grasp easily. A guy who's made millions of dollars in the widget-manufacturing business doesn't necessarily know from Ginnie Mae pass-throughs and closed-end funds. He needs you to make sense out of it."

Social work, which might seem on the surface to be the polar opposite of high finance, demands similar skills. Sarah Boehmler is senior vice president of marketing at the American Stock Exchange. But her first job after graduating from Sweet Briar

College in the late sixties was as a social worker in her native North Carolina.

"Now, I know that sounds like a surprising way to start out, but it taught me a lot about selling—about getting across a point of view in the most persuasive manner," she says. "I used to have to testify in child-custody cases, and I'd be cross-examined on which parent should get custody of a child, and it was crucial to be convincing under pressure, and make sure the child went to the right one.... And then sometimes I would have to try to persuade a child who had been taken out of his home for one reason or another to go to a foster home. Well, that is possibly the hardest sell in the world. That job made me attuned to people." After a couple of years, Sarah transferred those skills to business: she became the first female stockbroker licensed in North Carolina.

Davia Temin, too, has found that selling is selling, whether in academe or on Wall Street. In her seven years at Columbia Business School before joining Scudder, Stevens & Clark, Davia didn't earn an M.B.A.: she was hired in 1979 to start up a marketing department, as a way of attracting first-rate students and faculty who might otherwise have gone to Harvard, Stanford, or Wharton. "But, while I was there, I went to every single program and activity Columbia B-School *had*," she says with a laugh. "The dean told me I had an M.B.A. three times over." She has found that selling a school is not so different from selling the services of an investment-counseling firm. "Columbia, or any university, is essentially a stable of experts—fonts of knowledge, sources of information and insight. Well, an investment firm is in some ways the same thing. In both cases, you're promoting expertise and talent." The only real difference, she might have added, is the pay.

THE ROUGH-AND-TUMBLE of currency trading is, of course, another world. To be good at it, notes Berisford trader Sarah Gopher-Stevens, you need "a strong stomach and strong nerves." Born and raised in Holon, near Tel Aviv, Sarah came by those job qualifications in a way that most Americans would consider anything *but* "women's work." She was a sergeant in the Israeli Air Force during the Yom Kippur War.

Settled on a leather couch in a corner office down the hall from the trading room, Sarah talks about her life in a quiet, Hebrew-accented voice. She is thin, bony. She looks fragile. Except for her eyes: they are the flat bluish gray of gunmetal and, when she isn't smiling, easily as hard. She tells you this:

"Once I went in a Jeep, with an officer, to the Suez Canal. On our way back, when we had found out what we needed to know, the Jeep broke down. When it gets dark in the Sinai Desert, all you can hear is the wind. Just the wind screaming in the dark. There is nothing else there. We thought no one would come and look for us. At the base, we were not registered as having left." A long pause. "They did come and look for us, though. They told us, 'We thought probably you drove over a mine.' We were out there six hours, which is not very long. It felt like...maybe six days. Because of the wind.

"It changes you. It toughens you. You join the military in Israel —everyone has to—when you're eighteen, you're just a kid, and come out when you're twenty or twenty-one. And you're a different person when you come out. Five weeks of basic training. Living in tents in January. You assemble and disassemble and shoot guns, and you run miles and miles every day, and you clean latrines.

"Women are usually made into clerical staffers. I got assigned to do five weeks of classroom training instead. After that I was assigned to the electronic warfare unit. It was called that because we used electronic monitoring systems and communications systems. And airplanes and other weapons were activated electronically from our center." She stops for a second or two. "We decided all the time whether to send bombers.

"Often during the '73 war we were on the line and sent units on air missions. I knew these people. And our planes would be shot down. You know about it as soon as it happens. First the silence. Then another plane notifies you. The sensation in the pit of your stomach. It's . . . it's difficult.

"Anything the air force did, my unit was involved. Deciding whether to act. Sometimes at night I would be the only person there, and there was no time. There was no time to think and make a long, reasoned decision.

"On the very first day of the war, Yom Kippur 1973, one of our field units was in an area the Syrians invaded first. These were my friends, in this unit. We got radio calls: 'They are invading the bunkers now.' And then nothing. You knew your friends were dead.

"But there was always another decision to make, and then another one. . . . It gives you a different perspective. What's important, and what's not important. How to stay very calm under pressure, when everything seems to be going against you."

Her military experience has served Sarah well in other ways, too. Around the trading floor at Salomon she is remembered, with respect and affection, as "the sarge." She says with a little chuckle, "Wall Street is not a place that welcomes softies. I'll tell you one thing the air force was good for: it got me used to hearing people swear all day long. Yelling and swearing is a big part of some traders' style. It doesn't bother me at all, but personally I don't think it does anything for you. Most of the time, people are screaming at their own floor clerks, over at the Exchange or in Chicago, when something goes wrong. I'd rather sit down at the end of the day and try to discuss the problems more calmly." She pauses, clarifies: "Not that I *never* swear, but—it's very tame."

Sarah's past has given her reason to see not only Wall Street but New York and all of America with a kind of awe. "I love New York," she says, fervently enough to erase any ad-slogan overtones. "In Israel, everyone knows everyone. It's like a big family. Everywhere you go, someone knows someone who knows you. But in New *York!*" Sarah shakes her head, marveling: eight million strangers. "You can be anonymous, you can mingle in the crowd.

And have your own style, and be your own weird person, and no one minds.

"California was fine, the weather was like Israel; but you know, I could not relate to the people there. In New York I felt much more at home, immediately. The pace, the rhythm of the city, is like Tel Aviv. I also like Washington and Boston. I may never really be an American, but in these cities I'm not as foreign as I would be in Omaha, Nebraska." She says it as one long word: "Omahanebraska."

Unlike most New Yorkers, Sarah has actually been to Omaha. After business school at Stanford, she and a classmate drove across the country. "We wanted to see as much as we possibly could in the few weeks we had. We stopped in Cheyenne, Wyoming. That is one place I'd like to go back to. Someday my husband and I are going to buy a camper and take three months or six months, and drive everywhere and see everything."

Sarah gives out an ardent little sigh. "America is really wonderful, you know. I think Americans take it for granted a little bit, don't you think so? But America is like Wall Street." How is that? Sarah looks surprised at the question. "Well," she says, "they are two places where you can start new. And then have a fresh adventure every day." Ah. Obviously. Of course. Yes.

Nor is Sarah the only female Wall Streeter to have found a haven from political strife at home. Lilia Clemente, a first-rate money manager, has also turned her extraordinary background to unique financial advantage. While most of the rest of Wall Street took until the mid-eighties to discover financial life elsewhere on the planet, Lilia has made a career of studying economies and markets around the world for much longer. "These days you hear a lot about 'globalization,' " she observes. "I started thinking globally in 1969."

That year, at age twenty-eight, Lilia took on the job of co-managing investment research for the Ford Foundation's $3 billion portfolio of investments, the first woman to do so. Seven years later, she started her own company, Clemente Capital, Inc. Besides managing $150 million in clients' money, most of it invested in Japanese and other Asian stock markets, Lilia began to put out a monthly newsletter called the *Clemente Asian/Pacific Report*. Its purpose was, and still is, to keep subscribers abreast of political, social, and economic trends that could affect their Far Eastern holdings.

From the start, some of her competitors suspected she might be on to something. An article about her in *The Asian Wall Street Journal* in early 1981 quoted André Sharon, a senior analyst at Drexel Burnham Lambert: "She is zeroing in on some of the world's most attractive markets, with more growth potential and less tendency toward inflation than the U.S. or Western Europe. She could be the right person with the right product at the right time."

The right time rode in on the bull market, and Lilia's patient years of research paid splendid dividends. Starting in 1983, she ran the Atlas Fund, a PaineWebber mutual fund that puts investors' money into stocks in eighteen countries. In the first six months of 1986 alone, net asset value per share rose a glittering 84 percent from the previous year, making Atlas far and away the number-one global fund on Wall Street. Naturally, word got around, thanks partly to an enthusiastic write-up in *Money* magazine: Atlas brought PaineWebber more than $100 million in new client commissions. Suddenly, Lilia became something of a celebrity. "Now a lot of people want to analyze how I pick stocks," she says with a broad, sunny smile. "But I've been very Asian about it. Very mysterious. I keep my numbers very close to my chest."

After a couple of years at PaineWebber, Lilia missed her old independence and went back out on her own. In 1988 her firm formed a partnership called Clemente Global Investors. Thirty-five affluent individual investors, disheartened with domestic stocks, committed $150,000 each to the venture, which concentrates on snapping up undervalued issues in Thailand, Malaysia, Korea, and Japan. Clemente's global savvy also attracted the unwelcome enthusiasm of one surpassingly rich and famous investor, T. Boone Pickens III, son of the raider, who spent a good part of the summer of 1988 trying unsuccessfully to take over another of her ventures, Clemente Global Growth Fund, a closed-end mutual fund that trades on the Big Board in New York. Lilia fought off his advances and in 1989 began writing a book about the battle, to be published in Japan, where the Pickenses *père et fils* have become minor cult heroes.

Lilia came by her global perspective naturally. She was born and raised in Manila, where a legacy of colonialism, along with a steady influx of foreign capital and products, made her aware early of how commerce bursts across national boundaries. "You know, Spain ruled the Philippines, and then the U.S. 'liberated' us," Lilia tells you cheerily. "We Filipinos say: 'We spent 350 years in the convent and 50 years in Hollywood.'"

As a child, Lilia spoke both English and Tagalog, the native Philippine language; she was educated in schools run by American nuns. "Growing up in a mixed culture, especially one where so many consumer goods are imported from somewhere else, the children all develop a consciousness of exchange rates very young," she recalls. "We could do the calculations very fast in our heads. For instance, in high school I would go buy lipstick, and besides what color I would automatically ask myself, 'Hm, American or Japanese, what's the best value?'"

In one important respect, Lilia was hardly a typical child of her time and place. Her family, accomplished in business and prominent in politics, lived in aristocratic ease on a vast estate outside Manila. The only sign of political trouble in those days was a house on the grounds, tucked discreetly away from the main house, the guest house, and the servants' quarters, for the security staff— including both of Lilia's parents' full-time bodyguards. "Life was very comfortable there, with my parents and their ten cars and everything," Lilia remarks. "I was like one of my orchids, the ones I raise at home now—well watered and tended."

By the time she graduated from high school, Lilia was also a self-taught expert on, of all things, the world markets for nonferrous metals. Her father and grandfather were top executives and directors of the Philippines' two biggest mining companies, and Lilia took a shine to the business. While her friends spent their spare time on parties, clothes, and boys, Lilia was busy amassing and analyzing a hoard of information about international gold, silver, and copper prices and what makes them move. Her late mother saw nothing odd in that; but then, Belen Fabros Calderón was no stranger to unusual achievement. In 1964 she was elected the first woman governor of the Philippine province of Nueva Vizcaya, and she later became the first woman to hold a seat on the Manila Stock Exchange. After Lilia and her six siblings had grown and flown, their mother started and ran a Manila-based brokerage firm, A. J. Calderón Securities.

In that atmosphere, another Calderón daughter cultivated an esoteric skill, as well. Lilia's kid sister, María Teresa, now a teacher in Manila, became the world champion in speed-reading when she was fifteen years old. Tested at Northwestern University, María Teresa could read 80,000 words per minute, with 100 percent comprehension and recall. That record earned her a mention in the *Encyclopedia Britannica.*

Lilia came to the United States equipped with a bachelor's degree in business from the University of the Philippines and an undying fascination with the prices of metals. She earned a master's degree in economics, majoring in international trade, from the University of Chicago, and then did everything but her dissertation for a doctorate. "I loved being a student in Chicago," she says now. "I was poor, which was a new experience. Poor but happy." In 1966, CNA Financial Corp. hired her to manage a $300 million portfolio full of steel-company stocks and copper futures, so she moved to Pittsburgh. There, the locals seldom failed to ask whether she was related to Roberto Clemente, the Pittsburgh Pirates' star right-fielder. "I didn't even know who he was," she says. "They couldn't believe it!"

What she did know was metals. "As a mining analyst, I ran into lots of people who didn't expect me to know much. I was just this little tiny Filipino girl behind this great big desk," Lilia says now. "But when I would give a lecture on the global copper industry or something like that, they would be surprised. And they would sit up and listen."

Being a "tiny Filipino girl," Lilia believes, has in some respects helped her career rather than hindered it. "If you are not only foreign but female on top of it, you—and what you say—tend to stick in people's minds," she says. "They remember you because you're so *different.*"

Although she has lived in the States since 1960, Lilia is still a citizen of the Philippines. The political turmoil there has hit close to home. Her father, José Calderón, went to law school with Ferdinand Marcos and knew him well. But years afterward Calderón became a close political ally and advisor to Benigno Aquino, and served time in prison for his public criticism of the Marcos government.

On a small table in Lilia's office is a framed photograph of two middle-aged Filipino couples strolling on a placid tree-shaded street. The people in the picture are Lilia's parents and Benigno and Corazón Aquino, and they are walking to church in Amherst, Massachusetts, on a Sunday morning in August 1983. That same afternoon, Benigno Aquino boarded a plane for home. He was shot and killed when he arrived there. The assassination set in motion the two-and-a-half years of conflict that brought down the Marcos regime.

Of the People's Revolution, which put Corazón Aquino in power, Lilia says, beaming, "It was *beautiful.* I feel ten feet tall, I am so proud to be a Filipino. Because there was no bloodshed. Usually it is the military's job to protect the people. This time it was the other way around." The Calderóns, who had lived in exile in the United States from 1981 until 1988, returned to Manila. Lilia's father helped Cory Aquino reorganize the government after Marcos's departure, and her mother once again became the governor of

Nueva Vizcaya. Peace in the Philippines was tenuous and short-lived: guerrilla fighting soon resumed, and the Aquino democracy may yet be voted out of office or overthrown by force. Even so, hopes run high. Lilia says that after her parents arrived in the Philippines, they were so delighted to be home that they looked ten years younger.

As an afterthought, she murmurs: "Back in 1977, I got an award from Marcos: a big trophy, for being chosen as one of ten outstanding Filipinos. I still have it." She pulls aside a lush sheaf of foliage, and there is the trophy, two feet tall, gleaming on top of a radiator. "But I hide it over here behind these plants," she adds, *sotto voce*. And smiles.

LESS DRAMATIC, BUT no less significant for that, are the tales of women who came to Wall Street to escape not strife in other countries but sexism in other fields. Every few years, a special committee of the American Economic Association takes a hard look at how women economists are faring in the job market. In 1985, the committee's report noted that there were more of them around than ever before. A few statistics: women earned 34 percent of all bachelor's degrees in economics awarded by U.S. colleges, up from 22 percent in 1975; and 18 percent of all economics Ph.D.s in 1985 were women, up from 11 percent ten years earlier.

Female economists who want to teach in college do pretty well at the entry level, the study shows. In the same decade, the number of assistant professors who were women rose at about the same rate as the number of Ph.D.s. But, above the assistant-professor level, a curious thing happened. "Only 3 to 4 percent of all full professors were female in both 1975 and 1985," the report observed. "Progress to the top ranks of the profession has been slow or nonexistent."

Chase Manhattan's Leslie Daniels knows that only too well. It was the main reason she quit teaching. After a long day of chasing the ups and downs of the bond market, it's clear Leslie remembers the politics of academe only dimly and without rancor. She turns her enormous brown eyes on you and says evenly, "Women's track record at getting grants and promotions had been horrendous, yes. I admire any woman who sticks it out."

Leslie hung in there for seven years, first as an instructor at Stanford, where she earned her Ph.D.; and then, from 1977 to 1983, on the faculty of Washington University in St. Louis. "I was the first woman in the department at Washington in a tenure-track position. But I didn't have much hope of actually getting tenure."

Why not? Leslie sighs a silvery cloud of smoke. "Economics is still very much a male bastion, almost unbelievably so," she says. "I've given this a lot of thought, and I think the main reason for it is a kind of defensive attitude in the profession as a whole. Male economists don't want the field to be perceived as a 'soft' social science, like psychology or sociology. They have it in their heads that having women around in positions of influence would some-how make the whole discipline seem less 'serious' and 'scientific.' Another factor is that economics has become so much more quanti-tative than it used to be. There's a lot more math involved than there once was. And economists who are men really doubt any woman's ability to do analytical work, to be adept with numbers and sophisticated mathematical concepts."

Once she saw the handwriting on the blackboard, Leslie started casting around for a different line of work. "I'd done some consulting and enjoyed it tremendously. I wanted something where I could really use my analytical skills, either doing market analysis or maybe government policy–related work," she recalls. As it hap-pened, her husband Chuck, also an economics professor, was offered a teaching position at Fordham University. So in 1983 they moved to New York.

Her timing was terrific: most of the major New York commer-cial banks, always big employers of economists, were just then leaping headlong into the investment-banking fray. Moreover, they didn't all share academics' doubts about whether women could crunch numbers. "It was," Leslie says, "just perfect."

More than a few women were moved to try Wall Street by the abstract idea, back in the early days of feminism, that—surprise! —they were capable of doing anything if they wanted it badly enough. Before Leslie Christian arrived at Salomon Brothers in 1979, the firm didn't have a futures department. She was hired in 1979 to start it up. Over the ensuing decade, it became a billion-dollar business.

With a prim, no-nonsense air about her, and her short, straight hair specked with early gray, Leslie could be a small-town English teacher. But then that's fitting: she started her career teaching English in a junior high school in Tacoma, Washington. "It was 1969. Most women still believed they *had* to be either teachers or nurses," she says with a sardonic smile. "To tell you the truth, what I really expected was to be married and have two babies by age twenty-five. That was the other part of the status quo."

Then Leslie discovered the women's movement. For her, one book—Germaine Greer's landmark feminist essay *The Female Eunuch*—was the start of a different idea of life. "I remember reading it when it first came out and being *floored* by it," she says now. "Absolutely stunned. And I remember thinking, 'Yes, this is it, this is *true.*' So I decided to stop hanging around waiting to get married, and go to make my own way in the world." She did, starting with a stint at a savings bank in Seattle and an M.B.A. from Berkeley.

Somewhat ironically, other women were wooed to Wall Street by securities firms' efforts to redress their own past or present sexist ways. C. Austin Fitts, the municipal-bond whiz who became Dillon, Read's first female managing director in 1985, originally had her eye on the restaurant business. At the age of eighteen, just out of high school in her native Philadelphia, she went off to Hong Kong and managed a couple of nightclubs for a year or so. Austin is very likely the only partner, past or present, anywhere on Wall Street who speaks Mandarin Chinese and has trekked across Asia, from Hong Kong to Istanbul, with nothing but a knapsack.

At one point in her trans-Asian journey, the novelist John Fowles may have saved Austin's life, in a manner of speaking. In Calcutta, she was staying at a hostel run by the Salvation Army. One morning, lying on her bunk there, immersed in Fowles's *The French Lieutenant's Woman,* she remembered that she had promised a friend she would try a particular kind of dumpling sold in Calcutta's main marketplace. She went out to get it. "But I kept thinking about *The French Lieutenant's Woman.* It's a terrific story, and I was almost at the end, and I *really* wanted to see what was going to happen next. So I hurried. And then on my way back I stopped off at a jewelry shop, near the dumpling place, where I had been haggling with the owner over the price of a star sapphire I wanted, and we bargained a little more—but I *really wanted* to finish *The French Lieutenant's Woman.* So I left."

When she had gotten fifty yards down the street, walking fast, an explosion roared through the marketplace, killing the dumpling seller and injuring everyone in the jewelry shop. "It was a bomb planted by people on one side of a big labor dispute going on in India then," she recalls. "And if it hadn't been for that book . . . "

After that journey, she went back to Hong Kong and ran a bar called Thingummy's for a year. "I was also going to school. I owned two motorcycles. It was a great life," she says, a little dreamily. It also was not irrelevant to her later life on Wall Street. "I learned a lot about what it is to be an American. The Chinese really think very differently than we do. The Chinese and English languages reflect very different values." Austin pauses for a moment, reflecting, and then goes on: "I don't think it's possible to realize how materialistic our culture is until you have lived in a society that isn't but that provides a great sense of openness and community instead.

"And *logic.* I was brought up to think that it's important to win arguments in a logical way, and do everything for a logical reason. These are very deeply ingrained ideas in Western culture. But in

China intuition is given a lot more credit, as being a valid way of thinking or deciding. After a while, in an intellectual atmosphere that's so different, your sense of what's important changes. You acquire a new way of *looking*."

Intuition—in the form of a feeling about the stock market's next move, or a leap of judgment about whether or how to do a deal—is a treasured commodity on Wall Street. Everybody talks about it, and ponders where it comes from. Austin discovered hers, and began to cultivate it, on the other side of the world. "Most of my credit analysis has been based, at least initially, on an intuitive judgment," she says. "Of course, then somebody needs to do the research and put together the facts and the numbers to confirm it."

That sort of synthesis is part of the reason why investment bankers work in teams of two or three or four or more. Somebody is good at conceptual breakthroughs; somebody else crunches numbers adroitly; a third person might add a fillip the other two overlooked. In Austin's case, the original intuitive decision most often stands: the research turns out to support it.

At nineteen she went home and earned a degree in history from the University of Pennsylvania, working in a series of bars and restaurants all the while. After she graduated, she took a job managing the bar in a restaurant near the Penn campus called La Terrace. "One of my best customers was the dean of admissions at Wharton," she recalls. "He convinced me I ought to go to business school."

She took his advice, in 1976. But she still wasn't thinking of Wall Street—and might never have considered it, if Goldman, Sachs hadn't come along. In 1977, the firm was in the midst of one of its periodic fits of contrition over its failure to hire and promote more women. Accordingly, Goldman sent a letter to each and every first-year student at Wharton who happened to be female, offering interviews for a summer internship program at the firm. "People had been accusing them again of discriminating against women, so they were going all out," Austin notes. "Their recruiters asked me if I was interested in investment banking. I said no. But they kept calling me back for more interviews anyway. And then the more Goldman people I talked to, the more interested I got. I was very lucky." And so, it may be added, was Dillon, Read. Her interest in finance piqued by a summer at Goldman, Austin joined Dillon, Read after graduating from Wharton, and, by 1986, had turned the latter firm's municipal-bond department into one of the most vigorous muni operations on the Street.

OCCASIONALLY, women have been driven to come to Wall Street, and then to succeed here, by desperate necessity. Consider, for instance, Judy Connolly's story.

Even she admits that her rise to the ranks of the newly rich sounds like something out of a Judith Krantz novel. She was born in the Bronx to immigrant parents, her mother Russian, her father Austrian. "They came here during the Depression, when teachers were practically the only people who had jobs. If you were a teacher, you traveled to Europe, you were wealthy. So they said to me, 'Be a teacher, you'll always be secure.'" Judy laughs. "They never told me I was going to starve." After four years at Cornell, Judy earned two master's degrees, one in English and one in education, from Hunter College and Long Island University, respectively. She taught emotionally disturbed children for a few years, then switched to fifth-graders in a public school. She also married and had two sons.

It was what she, and her parents, had always wanted. Until the unthinkable happened: her husband, in a horrific car accident, suffered severe, irreversible brain damage. His hospital bills took all their savings, and Judy abruptly found herself the family's sole support. On her small teaching salary, life was bleak. "We lived in subsidized housing for a while; we were really *poor*," she says now, her voice cracking a little. "I'll tell you what I remember most. We had a dog, and one day he ate my only pair of shoes. I couldn't afford another pair. I sat down and cried. Then I pulled myself together and said, 'All right, enough already.' And I swore I would never be that broke again. Never."

Still, it didn't occur to her to try Wall Street until a friend suggested it. "I was doing secretarial work in the summers for the extra money, and a friend of mine who runs an employment agency told me about an opening at Merrill Lynch, at headquarters all the way downtown. I wasn't wild about the idea. I lived on Roosevelt Island, and the thought of taking the Lexington Avenue subway all the way down there in the summer with all those people packed in there sweating all over you . . . !" Judy wrinkles her nose, laughing. "But I took it. At first I was working for a lawyer. I was supposed to be proofreading stuff I didn't even understand. It was crazy."

Judy's second boss at Merrill Lynch was in the corporate-finance department, and it was he who inadvertently got her started as a broker. One evening he took her along to dinner at Delmonico's with four executive vice presidents from Chemical Bank, who wanted to discuss a deal. "I was supposed to be writing everything down, and I don't take shorthand. And I didn't understand what they were talking about," Judy recalls, flushing with remembered agitation. "But I'm writing and writing and writing. All through drinks and appetizers and the main course, I'm writing, I'm writing. Then my boss stands up and says, 'Well, I have to go now, I'm catching a plane to Chicago. Judy, you take care of this.' And he *leaves.*" Judy gives a little gasp, and a sputter of laughter. "I was in shock.

"So I turned to these guys and I said, 'Look, I have to level with you. I can't even write fast enough to get all this down and I don't know what the hell it's all about. I'm a *secretary.* But if you play straight with me, I'll try my best to make sure we do this business with you, whatever it is.' By that time we were on dessert. And we sat there and talked for a long time. Hours."

That particular deal never came off, but the bankers didn't forget Judy. When, a couple of years later, she passed the licensing examinations to qualify as a broker, one of those men handed her a Chemical Bank account worth $35 million. "That was my first big account," Judy says, beaming. "That's how I got started. Somebody has to *believe* in you." She throws another quick look at her computer screen. "A couple of my first clients trusted me with millions of dollars, before I had any real experience at all, which I *told* them. But they thought I could do it."

Like many women of her generation, raised to be self-effacing if not self-deprecating, Judy shrugs off the credit for her own success. Becoming one of the top Merrill Lynch brokers in the United States, to hear her tell it, was largely a matter of being in the right place at the right time. But one of her bosses, a high-ranking Merrill Lynch executive who calls her "without a doubt one of the very best people we have," tells this story: "Judy used to come into the office every day at 7 a.m., long before anybody else showed up. One morning the phone was ringing off the hook and there was no one else here to answer it, so she picked it up. It was a woman screaming and carrying on, saying she couldn't understand her account statement. She thought there was a terrible error in it and she wanted help with it right away. She was furious. She wasn't Judy's client, but Judy told her, 'Hang on, I'll be right over.' She grabbed her coat and ran off to this woman's apartment to explain her statement to her. Today that woman is one of our biggest clients. Judy will tell you, 'Oh, I was just lucky, I happened to be there when she called.' But luck has nothing to do with it. Judy has made her own luck." Mention this to Judy and she says, "Well, let's just say I'm a great believer in the American Dream."

So is Susan Byrne. Like Judy, Susan made her way on Wall Street, eventually founding and running multi-million-dollar Westwood Management, because she felt she *had* to. Indeed, Susan looks back on her career with a certain incredulity. Picking at a salad in a noisy midtown steakhouse, she recalls that, when she was growing up in California, she had expected to spend her life taking care of a husband and children, engaged in no financial task more risky or complicated than balancing the joint checking account. "I was brought up very traditionally. I never thought I would have a career at all. I majored in history at Berkeley, but I didn't graduate. And the last math I ever took was in high school, when I dropped the second half of Algebra II. I had no incentive to keep it up. I mean, I was a cheerleader, and my social life was more important to me than anything else."

Susan still looks like the stereotypical "California girl," and it isn't hard to picture her as a cheerleader, being true to her school just as the Beach Boys said she should in that song that was always playing on the radio. As a matter of course, she married early and had a baby a year later. But the marriage broke up almost at once, and Susan found herself in New York, with a small son to support, when she was still in her early twenties.

"So I started working, naturally. But, as I was struggling along, I remember thinking of it as a temporary thing. I thought of the jobs I had as no more than ways of surviving until my *real* life worked out." Susan takes a tiny bite of unbuttered bread and flashes you an ironic grin. "I was well into my thirties before I realized, hey, this is a career. I'm not just between marriages here."

If she started out without much ambition for herself, Susan did have a child to consider. "In my own mind, I could cope with getting ahead, and making more and more money, by telling myself that I was doing it for my son. So I worked hard. And I was incredibly pushy. I pushed much harder than I would have if I had been responsible only for myself. It's amazing, looking back, that so many people suffered me as gracefully as they did. But, on the other hand, this business does reward people who push hard. And who are willing to risk biting off more than they can chew."

Susan's first job on Wall Street was as a secretary at E. F. Hutton, but she soon pushed her way into an editing slot in the firm's research department, a job she describes as "taking the security analysts' reports and turning them into something resembling English." In 1971, William Witter, a topnotch investment research boutique that has since been acquired by Drexel Burnham Lambert, offered her a higher salary to do the same thing, so she went there. It was a crucial move. "I learned economics and finance at Witter, because my way of editing analysts was to make sure I understood *every* word in their reports before I picked up a pencil," she says. "So I had some of the brightest people in the business explaining to me in detail what they were thinking and why. They were very patient. Very generous. They would recommend books and things for me to read, and I would study at night after my son was asleep, and they would answer any questions that I had."

Susan showed herself an exceptionally quick study, well worth the analysts' time. Within a year, she noticed a significant hole in Witter's research. When one of the firm's analysts misjudged the fate of a company's stock, it was most often because he or she had neglected to take into account some economic trend or political event that affected that company's sales and earnings. One day, CBS's stock price took a steep dive, and nobody could figure out why. Witter's broadcasting-industry analyst hadn't a clue, and CBS wouldn't comment. Susan had the idea of checking to see what might be going on in Washington. Sure enough, it turned out that a vociferous congressional subcommittee was holding hearings on TV advertising aimed at children. CBS executives were taking a shellacking from indignant lawmakers; and canny investors, concerned about possible restrictions on a major source of CBS revenues, were dumping the stock.

"So I told our analyst about it, and it gave him a little bit of an edge," Susan recalls. "I had always been interested in politics, and very aware of political issues, since my Berkeley days." The CBS incident, and others like it, prompted Susan to propose a new research service that would meld political and regulatory consid-erations into Witter's financial data. It's a facet of security analysis that has since become second nature on the Street, but at that moment in the early seventies, no other firm had yet thought of doing it in any systematic way. Robert Gabel, then Witter's director of research and Susan's boss, liked the idea: "He went to bat for me and got approval from upstairs, so I went ahead with it."

Two years later, Susan gained a second mentor when Charles O'Hay, an influential investment strategist, joined Witter and championed her efforts. "It was absolutely *critical* to have Charlie's seal of approval," she says now. "He would include me in presentations to important clients, and he always let me speak before he did. Those meetings exposed me to a level of management I normally never got to see. But the best part of it was I discovered I had a natural ability as an analyst. I was really good at picking stocks." Susan took her newfound confidence to Lehman Brothers, and then, in 1977, moved on to Bankers Trust—and her first job as a portfolio manager. By the time she accepted the assistant-treasurer post at GAF in 1980, she was a seasoned pro.

Didn't any of her employers object to the fact that she had never finished college? Stirring a cup of black coffee, Susan gives you a long, contemplative look before opting for candor. "Well," she finally says, unapologetically, "I wasn't always honest about it. I usually just let people *assume* I had graduated. But I knew I could do the work. And I needed the money. So I don't know what else I could have done, really."

THE LATEST GENERATION of Wall Street women, those who joined investment banks in the eighties while still in their twenties, followed a more straightforward route. Familiar almost from birth with the notion of equal opportunity, they didn't go off on detours into "women's work," or wrestle with the old "feminine" ambivalence about ambition. From a good college to a prestigious business school to a job on Wall Street—it's as natural a progression for them as for their male peers.

Without a doubt, that orthodoxy brings with it certain advantages. For one thing, having precisely the same credentials as the young men around them should remove at least one potential stumbling

block from the newcomers' upward path. Accustomed to competing on an equal footing, this generation of female financiers may
be more inclined to insist on equal pay.

"I've never squawked as much as maybe I should have, when
I knew I wasn't being paid as much as the guys were making, or
getting promoted as fast," admits one investment banker in her
late thirties. Before she earned an M.B.A. and came to Wall Street,
she had studied art history and then taught high-school French
for a couple of years. "Because of my background, I've always had
it in the back of my mind that, hey, things aren't fair around here,
okay — but I'm still a lot better off than I was before, as a teacher. If
I'd never done that, my attitude would have been completely
different, and my Wall Street career would probably have advanced
more quickly than it did."

At the same time, some veteran Wall Street women wonder if
female fledglings haven't been lulled into a false sense of equality.
With the Age of Reagan, much of the country hunkered down into
a politically conservative mindset that colored social attitudes,
too. "Feminism," like "liberalism," bid fair to become a dirty
word, even though, as with what became known as the "L-word,"
its detractors were usually hard put to define it. But if feminism is
nothing more, or less, than the chance to excel and the right to be
rewarded accordingly, then clearly women who came to Wall
Street straight from college and B-school in the eighties take it
very much for granted.

Perhaps they should not be so hasty. Linda Costello, the leveraged-buyout specialist at Dean Witter, observes that "very young
men — the ones who came to Wall Street in the eighties — have a sort
of macho conservatism about them that is a throwback, *not* to the
guys who are ten or fifteen years older than they are, but to their
fathers' generation. It's as if we're heading back to the 1950s all
over again." Other women agree. "Young women who haven't
been here very long have a wonderful optimism. But maybe they
just don't realize yet what they're going to be up against," says

Morgan Stanley analyst Brenda Landry. "Sure, they're equal to the guys *now*. But as they try to rise through the ranks, they may be in for a real shock." The more things change, according to this point of view, the more they stay the same.

By coming a long way round, earlier waves of women seem to have gained a singular perspective in other respects as well. A former teacher, or dancer, or social worker, or restaurant manager knows from firsthand experience that there is more to get up for in the morning than working an eighty-hour week and making pots of money. All kinds of other things matter: friends, family, ideas, art, politics, the whole world that lies beyond the green gaze of the Quotron screen. It's a view of life that can be particularly tonic in the event of some major setback at the office—such as, for instance, a stock-market crash.

Maybe because seasoned Wall Street women have had to struggle harder along the way than their younger sisters, and cope with more uncertainty, they seem to take a more genuine delight in their own success—a profound satisfaction mingled with a gleeful little bit of surprise. Susan Byrne speaks for many when she says, "This is not at all how my mother told me my life was going to be. But thank heavens it turned out this way."

IV.
THE SEARCH
FOR BALANCE

The Starlight Roof of the Waldorf-Astoria Hotel in Manhattan is a cavernous high-ceilinged ballroom, walled in tall etched-glass Art Deco panels, trimmed in gaudy gilt. On a weekday evening in late autumn of 1987, its mirror-smooth parquet floor slowly fills with prosperous-looking people, pink-cheeked from the cold outside, mostly dressed in formal black, mostly under forty. This crowd is paying $250 a head—$1,000, for those five hundred or so who are staying for dinner upstairs in the Jade Room—to sip cocktails with Michael and Kitty Dukakis and to hear a short, informal speech from the candidate, replete with homespun Greek wisdom. A typical aphorism, received by this group with hoots and applause: "The sweetest honey comes but slowly."

The glossy invitation to this party bore the names of Dukakis's New York fund-raising committee, most of whom are here tonight: actors Eli Wallach, Tony Randall, Shelley Winters, Maureen Stapleton; celebrity photographer Jill Krementz; former New Jersey governor Brendan Byrne; Senator Edward Kennedy. A few

Wall Streeters are listed too, among them mergers-and-acquisitions wizard Bruce Wasserstein. And, oh yes, a couple of Wall Street women—Barbara Shattuck, a partner in the firm of Cain Bros. Shattuck, Inc.; and Davia Temin of Scudder, Stevens & Clark. As the cocktail hour stretches on and the din of conversation gets steadily louder and more lively, both Davia and Barbara go mingling through the room, smiling and chatting and shaking hands. They and their fellow finance-committee members and co-chairmen have persuaded most of these eight hundred busy people to leave their offices a little early and fight for a cab in a frigid New York rush hour, in order to be here, have a drink or two, and stick "Dukakis for President '88" buttons into their silk or worsted-wool lapels. The evening is a clear success. By the end of it, the Dukakis campaign's coffers have been sweetened by at least $1 million.

For the most part, in the 1988 presidential election, Wall Street was Bush country. Striking evidence of that came on October 19, 1988, the first anniversary of Black Monday. On that day, the ever-spinning rumor mill put out the word that the Washington *Post* was set to publish a devastating story about George Bush's private life—something, it was thought, along the lines of the newspaper exposé that had quashed Gary Hart's Democratic candidacy eighteen months earlier. The Bush rumor, of course, turned out to be false. But the merest chance that it might not be, and that a Dukakis presidency loomed ahead, was enough to dampen the Dow by 34 points in a single afternoon.

An utterly impartial observer—if such could be found—might have been forgiven for wondering why. The naming of Dan Quayle as the Republican running mate gave rise to a flock of jokes on trading floors all over the Street. Some traders called Quayle "the ultimate zero-coupon bond: no maturity, no interest." Far more important, the three things financiers most love to hate are huge federal budget deficits, high interest rates, and stock market crashes. In the eighties, the Reagan-Bush administration helped give Wall Street the biggest budget deficits in U.S. history, the loftiest sustained real interest rates ever, and the most precipitous market plunge since 1929. Perhaps for those reasons, some illustrious Wall Streeters crossed over to the Dukakis cause. Two notable Democrats were Jerome Kohlberg, a partner in the leveraged-buyout powerhouse Kohlberg Kravis Roberts & Co., whose deal making had netted him an estimated $350 million; and Robert Bass, a Texas billionaire investor who wrote the Dukakis campaign a personal check for $100,000.

Many Wall Street women, mirroring the female voting population as a whole, leaned toward Dukakis, too. But they seemed motivated not by disillusion with the then-recent past but by worry about the future. For Barbara Shattuck, who worked for seven years in the public-finance department at Goldman, Sachs before starting her own firm with two partners who came from Morgan Stanley, politics had long been a priority. As a college student in the early seventies, she protested the Vietnam War—even though "my father didn't speak to me for eight months" as a result—and she has been a Democrat ever since. Fund-raisers like the one at the Waldorf, Barbara said, were "an opportunity to reach out to my peers, baby boomers who still have a social conscience and who aren't aligned now with any political party. A lot of these people are ripe to become Democrats, because they see the Republicans as 'the rich people's party.'"

Barbara is, of course, quite well-heeled herself. Still, she saw no irony in her position. "I am concerned," she said, "that there are a number of social issues, like cuts the Republicans have made in Medicare and Aid to Families with Dependent Children, that are easy to gloss over when the economy is relatively strong. In another economic downturn, these things will come to the fore again."

Davia Temin had reasons of her own for clambering aboard the Dukakis bandwagon. For one thing, she knows the man: he had been her boss for a couple of years in the seventies, when she worked in Massachusetts as the Governor's community-services specialist. "When somebody wanted to see Governor Dukakis, they usually saw me instead," she explains. "I dealt with everyone from a parent whose son was being mistreated in jail to somebody who had a quarrel with a public utility. It wasn't a glamorous job. It was just ironing out the ordinary problems that people have." That experience convinced Davia that Dukakis was "one of the neatest people I've ever met. He was an honest politician. And he really cared about his constituents."

Still impressed a decade later, Davia joined the Dukakis campaign on its triumphant ride across Pennsylvania during the presidential primaries, and devoted a few more of her vacation days to the Democratic National Convention, where Dukakis was formally nominated in July of 1988. Davia comes by her modestly leftward leanings honestly. A Quaker from Ohio, she retains an anti-materialistic streak. "I never lost a lot of my early idealism," she says. "I think it's really important to be committed to what you do with your time, and how you live your life, other than a 'lifestyle,' beyond just maintaining a certain financial standard of living."

Certainly some women on Wall Street are Republicans. One of them, Dillon, Read's Austin Fitts, served as a surrogate speaker for the Reagan campaign in 1984, addressing groups of professional women around New York in hopes of winning their votes for The Gipper. Her efforts, combined with her remarkable Wall Street record, didn't go unnoticed by Republican party leaders. In the spring of 1989, Secretary of Housing and Urban Development Jack Kemp chose Austin as an assistant secretary of the agency, with the added title of federal housing commissioner. She was nominated for the post by President Bush in late May. Even before her confirmation, Austin moved to Washington and began devoting sixteen-hour days to untangling the Reagan-era mess of corruption, mismanagement, and fraud at the Federal Housing Administration, which will cost at least $2 billion of the taxpayers' money to put right.

Yet even so estimable a Republican as Austin acknowledges that "most of the other women I know on Wall Street are Democrats, no matter *how* affluent they are. They know there are social problems a free market won't address, such as the fact that poverty is becoming more and more prevalent among women and children."

Austin's own choice of party seemed more practical than ideological. As a New Yorker, she had long observed that New York State has always been so heavily Democratic that both it and its biggest city get little attention from Washington when the White House is occupied by Republicans. "To be heard by any administration, and to be effective in Congress, you have to be able to work *both* sides of the aisle, not just the Democratic side," she said. "And I think the best thing for women to do is to keep plugging away at increasing our influence in both parties."

Whichever side of the aisle they favor, a surprising number of women on Wall Street seem to actively share Barbara Shattuck's view that "people need to get more involved in politics. Among people my age, in their thirties or forties, there is a tendency to be cynical and say, 'Oh, it doesn't matter, it doesn't mean anything,' and just sit back and do nothing," she observes. "Well, if we all sit back and do nothing, we're going to have real problems down the road."

IN SOME WAYS, Wall Street since the late seventies has been a kind of mercenary monastery, a haven for the bright but socially maladjusted. The killing hours and ceaseless demands of the money trade seem to attract a disproportionate number of people who, for reasons of their own, prefer to avoid entanglements in anything but work. In his novel *A Theft,* Saul Bellow observes that some people yearn to be, and succeed at being, "too influential to have a personal life. . . . High enough in the power structure, you can be excused from having one, an option lots of people are glad to exercise." Given how uncertain, messy, and painful a personal life can be—compared to the clear-cut, easily explicable wins and losses of the Wall Street workplace—the temptation to excuse oneself, for people of a certain temperament, is real.

But during the frantic bull-market years on Wall Street, and in some areas of investment banking and securities trading even afterward, what looked like apathy or avoidance may in large part have been simple exhaustion. Relentlessly hectic hours at work can drain away whatever energy might otherwise go to nobler or more heartfelt pursuits. Bond trader Leslie Daniels admits that, after ten straight hours of pumping adrenaline on the trading floor, all she wants to do is spend a few blessedly uneventful hours hanging around at home. "My idea of a big night is to crawl into bed and eat macaroni and cheese, or take-out Chinese, and watch middlebrow TV," she says with a wry laugh. "I wish I could tell you I spend my spare time tutoring disadvantaged children or something, but I don't. I do like to garden. And read. And *sleep*.

"They're solitary activities. When you're trading, you're sitting there at a desk with ten other people practically in your lap. In a hot market, there's a lot of shouting and swearing and carrying on. And you develop these strange, close relationships with brokers and dealers whom you know only as disembodied voices over the phone. So quiet and solitude become terribly important. Especially solitude."

At least as often, Wall Streeters find they crave the company of friends or family, but just can't fit it in. "When you're working on a deal—a merger or a leveraged buyout or whatever—you live at the office," says Morgan Stanley research analyst Brenda Landry. "And you lose friends sometimes. People who have regular nine-to-five jobs get tired of waiting for you. They give up calling after a while."

Brenda had her share of suitors, in her single days, who were made uncomfortable by her wealth; but she believes that an even bigger reason why Wall Street women so often marry men in the same line of work is that nobody else understands why it takes up so much time. "These hours can be hell on any relationship. You really need somebody who understands *why* you have to leave town on short notice, *why* you have to cancel social plans time after time, *why* your schedule is so crazy."

In 1980, when Brenda married a stockbroker who works at E. F. Hutton, she very nearly missed her own wedding, an elaborate black-tie affair that had taken months of planning in advance. When the big day rolled around, she was at her desk, rushing to finish a sixty-page research report on the photography industry: "I was the first photography analyst the firm ever had, you see, and it was just not a deadline that I could afford to blow."

Of course, once two extremely busy people have found a few minutes in which to say "I do," it means twice as many daily details get neglected. Neither one has time to go to the post office, or pick up dry cleaning, or pay bills, or renew the registrations on the cars. Indeed, so basic a task as picking up a few groceries becomes a challenge, and finding a way to entertain at home is out of the question. Says one female investment banker, who is married to an equally high-powered man in the advertising business: "Depending on whether the cleaning lady has been there lately, our place either looks fine or as if Sherman's army had slept there. And I never buy produce, I haven't bought lettuce in a year. We had a lot of penicillin in the vegetable bin before I finally gave up."

The alternative to giving up is hiring the most conscientious household help money can buy. It's a solution that only a woman with a queenly salary can afford. Worn to a frazzle by the pressures of her job at Dillon, Read, along with "shopping and cooking and cleaning and errands and entertaining and so on and so on and so on and *so* on," Austin Fitts explains, "I was going *mad.*" So she put a help-wanted ad in the *New York Times* and hired her Cordon Bleu helpmate, Anthony. "I gave him a twenty-page job description," she says. "And he made a very good salary. He was an absolute lifesaver."

Under these conditions, it isn't hard to understand why many Wall Street women don't have children. Ask Laurie Hawkes at Salomon Brothers whether she thinks she'll have any and she answers, half seriously, "Oh, gosh, I don't know. Can you carry a baby around in a briefcase?" Still in her early thirties, Laurie has time to make up her mind. But, notes one of her colleagues, the possibility tends to get more remote as the years speed by. "In this line of work there never seems to be a good time to stop for a while and have a child. There is no such thing as part-time work on Wall Street. And leaving, even for a couple of months, is risky. You can find yourself out of it so quickly," says this observer, a woman who speaks from experience. "So you tend to say, yes, yes, of course, I do want kids. But not right now. And you go on that way until it's too late."

Once they decide to take the plunge, female Wall Streeters who do have children struggle to find time for them. "There is really no way you can be someone's mother and be away twelve or fourteen hours a day," observes Susan Lipton, an attorney in corporate finance at L. F. Rothschild, whose daughter was born in 1985. "What you end up doing is delegating the mothering to a nanny and become a kind of second father." Even more than most other mothers who work outside the home, Wall Street women are torn by conflicting loyalties because they so often work around the clock. "If by some miracle you ever find yourself with a free hour," says an investment banker at Morgan Stanley who has a small son, "you ask yourself, 'Okay, where do I want to spend this hour? On my child? Myself? My husband? My career?' The answer is never simple or clear—and anyway, it's only *one hour*. So it's easy to feel after a while as if you are just not doing a good enough job at any of it."

Those brave enough to start families rely on varying strategies for making it all fit together. One of these is hiring full-time, round-the-clock nannies. Another is deliberately making a point of *not* doing so. American Stock Exchange senior vice president Sarah Boehmler and her husband, a former investment banker who is now an executive at International Paper Corp., have three daughters. When they come home from school, the girls are with their governess. But this nanny doesn't live in: Sarah and her husband decided at the start that they wanted help only until about 6:30 in the evening. "This way," Sarah explains, "one of us *has* to be home by then. Otherwise, you see, it would be too easy to get caught up in work and meetings and so on until past the children's bedtime. And end up with no family life at all."

Then too, there is the occasional weekend. Joyce Fensterstock, the PaineWebber managing director who oversees many of the firm's mutual funds and its merchant-banking operations, tries to set aside as many weekends as she can for quiet time with her two sons and her husband, at the family's house in the country. Even so, she worries: "Sometimes I think when they're thirteen and fifteen years old, they'll stay out all night and tell me, 'I didn't come home, why should I? *You* weren't there when I was three-and-a-half and fell off the jungle gym.' But then I think, when *I* was thirteen, my complaint was that my mom was there all the time and wouldn't let me grow up on my own ... so ... no matter what you do ... it's difficult. But the joy is well worth it."

After years of raising a child all on her own, Susan Byrne became accustomed to carving out time for her home life: "As a single parent, you have to make time. You don't have a choice, with this little guy depending on you." Now that he's away at college, she says, "I refuse to fill up that time with work! I don't want my life to be that unbalanced. It's important to me to know that I am a person above and beyond running my company. The company is what I do. It's not who I am." A subscriber to myriad theater, ballet, and opera companies, Susan sees some kind of performance three or four nights a week, and she's become a fixture at art-history lectures at the Metropolitan Museum. At her summer place on Long Island, she's learning how to play golf.

During the eighties, as greater-than-ever numbers of young women arrived on Wall Street with brand-new M.B.A. degrees in hand, the perennial conflict between work and family caused widespread alarm—even, or perhaps especially, among single women, whose jobs left them no time to meet potential mates.

Anxiety reached a crescendo in June of 1986, when *Newsweek* printed an article with the ominous title "Too Late for Prince Charming?" The story cited a study, by a group of sociologists from Harvard and Yale, which indicated that college-educated women who were still unwed at age thirty stood only a 20 percent chance of ever marrying at all. At thirty-five, the study said, the chance was even slimmer, at 5 percent. And at forty—forget about it. "Forty-year-olds are more likely to be killed by a terrorist," *Newsweek* remarked. "They have a minuscule 2.6 percent probability of tying the knot."

The *Newsweek* bombshell was given sensational play on TV news shows, not to mention in countless frantic long-distance phone calls from millions of worried moms. On Wall Street, where many young bull-market-driven women had no time to sleep, let alone date, the whole affair set off what one female trader recalls as "shock waves. Suddenly we all looked up and said, '*Whoa.* What are we doing with our lives, here? Is this really worth it?' "

For some, the answer has been an emphatic "no." Lynn Ingalls (yes, she is related to the Laura Ingalls Wilder who wrote *The Little House on the Prairie*—Lynn is the author's grandniece) started her merchant-banking career at Shearson Lehman Hutton in 1986. She left two years later. Why? "I wasn't willing to marry my job," she says. In her second year at Shearson, she saw one five-month stretch in which she managed to take only a single day off; and never once in the other 149 days did she get home before midnight. "I was canceling nine out of ten dates," she recalls. "Or, really, more like ten out of ten. I wanted to get married and have a family and, at that rate, it just wasn't ever going to happen."

Lynn still does merchant banking, including elaborate bridge-loan and junk-bond financings for leveraged buyouts. But she's now doing it for the Rockefeller Group, a small private start-up that in 1988 did six deals ranging in size from $60 million to $1 billion. The main difference is, at this firm she works only about fifty hours a week, and thus can squeeze in a social life. "The money I'm earning here is less than I'd be making if I'd stayed on Wall Street," she says, "but that's okay with me. I like working for an organization where it's accepted that there is more to life than just work."

WHETHER THEY ESPOUSE political causes, have children, or direct their nonprofessional energies toward other ends, women have always been more anxious than their male peers on Wall Street to avoid being totally absorbed by their jobs.

Indeed, the tendency to want something — even just a *little* something, once in a while — out of life, above and beyond a fast-track career, has often been held against women in their quest for respect and promotion at the office. After all, the investment banker who hasn't got a traditional wife at home taking care of things, as most successful male financiers have, might be distracted at some crucial moment by — imagine it! — domestic matters.

She may even want or need a little time off now and then. "Women are definitely more inclined to see ourselves as people apart from our careers, to define ourselves in part by other aspects of our lives," notes Heather Evans, a Harvard M.B.A. who has worked at Morgan Stanley and Bear Stearns. "And men do see it as a problem, if we seem to give our families or other interests a higher priority than the guys around us do."

Yet, despite that resistance, and in the face of almost overwhelming day-to-day logistical odds, Wall Street women cling to the notion that life is a many-splendored thing. Perhaps it's because they see the meaning of money in quite different terms, or because they gained insights into the outside world by first pursuing other, less narrowly focused careers. Perhaps it's simply that most women were raised from an early age to believe that it's healthier to lead a well-rounded life, and make time for matters of the heart and the intellect as well as the wallet, and they've never quite gotten rid of the idea. But, whatever their individual reasons, Wall Street women as a group are markedly wary of coming to resemble Rex Mottram, a shrewd and greedy character in Evelyn Waugh's novel *Brideshead Revisited.* Mottram, in Waugh's words, "isn't a real person at all; he's just a few faculties of a man highly developed." Or, as money manager Lilia Clemente puts it: "If you end up like a bonsai tree and stop growing, you're in trouble."

Some women choose outside pursuits that take them as far from Wall Street's pressures as it's possible to go, and still be within a weekend's driving distance. Kristin Gamble, a partner in the money-management firm Flood, Gamble Associates, owns a thirty-five-acre farm in upstate New York. She and her husband grow beets, carrots, onions, tomatoes, and beans, and harvest apples, peaches, and raspberries. They also board horses and cows for neighboring farmers. As her various crops come into season, Kristin pickles, cans, and preserves them all. She has even taught a course, at an adult-education center in Manhattan called the Learning Annex, on the gentle, homespun art of making jams and jellies. "It's a tremendous pleasure to keep in touch with the changing seasons this way, and to watch things grow," Kristin says. "Farming is the best way I can imagine to get completely away from the daily grind." It is also a return to her family's roots: Kristin's forebears many generations ago were Swedish farmers who crossed the Great Plains in covered wagons to Nebraska, where she grew up.

By contrast, other Wall Street women opt for activities that are almost as competitive and results-oriented as their jobs are. Amy Lane, a principal in mergers and acquisitions at Morgan Stanley, was the inventor of an imaginative strategy that let client Union Carbide fight off a hostile $4.8 billion takeover attempt by GAF Corp. in the first two months of 1986. Amy's ploy, a complicated method of exchanging debt for stock so as to make a takeover target look abruptly less appetizing to a would-be acquirer, has become a staple in the m&a business, and she is justifiably proud of it. She shrugs off the price she paid: several weeks of nonstop work and worry, including a Christmas Day spent crunching numbers at the office. "It's a real kick," she says. "It's *fun*. And, in order to get anywhere in this business, you have to feel that way. You have to like it." Still, Amy has never let work get in the way of her golf game. She won the annual golf championship at her country club in New Jersey every year for fourteen summers running. With a handicap of 2, she was featured in *Fortune* magazine as one of the best executive golfers—male or female— in the United States.

In an era when every new book of advice for business people warns ambitious managers of the damage that too much stress can do to their careers—and cardiologists chime in with well-documented caveats of their own—the mercilessly macho climate of Wall Street has sometimes made the place seem like the last retrograde bastion of do-or-die workaholism. That is curious, even downright irrational, since an occasional break can do wonderful things for a person's productivity. Far from detracting from performance at the office, some extracurricular activities seem to help sharpen the skills and strengthen the confidence that are useful in any high-pressure job.

Sarah Boehmler, for one, has spent much of her scarce spare time rolling with some punches that would make most people blanch. Every now and then, she leaves her job and family behind and heads off into the wilderness on an expedition led by an outfit called Outward Bound. Now twenty-seven years old, Outward Bound began in the Colorado Rockies and later moved its headquarters to Connecticut. The organization is an offshoot of a program begun in Wales during World War II to help merchant seamen survive German torpedo attacks by teaching them teamwork, self-confidence, and resourcefulness under fire. Five Outward Bound schools around the United States offer rafting, hiking, skiing, and horseback-riding trips that claim more than sixty thousand alumni, some of whom were sent into the wilderness by their employers. Big corporations, including IBM and Xerox, have found that a prolonged hand-to-hand tussle with Mother Nature brings out some useful qualities in managers, and toughens them up.

The trips are no day at the beach. They're designed, in fact, to be as grueling as possible, within certain limits; Outward Bound apparently means to test people's mental and physical endurance to the point of terror and despair, while still endeavoring to make sure that they come back in one piece.

Sarah's first experience with Outward Bound, in 1980, was a rafting trip down the Chattooga River in North Carolina. Yes, that is the harrowing river that runs through the novel *Deliverance*. "James Dickey said once that he wished he'd never written that book, because so many people saw the movie and then some of them went and drowned, trying to imitate it," Sarah remarks off-handedly. "It really doesn't *look* so bad, but there are vortexes in the Chattooga that will drag your body down so that it will never even be found. It is not a trip for amateurs."

Sarah's fellow amateurs included some chief executive officers of companies whose shares are listed on the Amex and a couple of high-ranking executives from Wall Street securities houses. She recalls, "Afterward, one of the men turned to me and said that his whole attitude about women on Wall Street had changed, because he saw that I could keep up. And in fact, at several times I wasn't as frightened as some of the men were, or if I was I handled it, I didn't get hysterical. I kept going. He said it made him wonder whether he had overlooked some women at the office because he had been assuming that they weren't strong enough to handle pressure."

A year later, Sarah embarked on another Southern river sojourn, this time on the Green. Its itinerary included a fair amount of what mountain climbers call rappelling, and other people call crazy. One morning, the group's Outward Bound leader roused everyone from their sodden woodland beds at dawn. "It was a *fantastic* view, as the sun came up, of all the distant mountains," Sarah says. "But we were standing on the edge of a cliff. And it was a sheer drop to the bottom. A couple of hundred feet. We had to back off the mountain. That is, we had to jump off—backward, with nothing but a skinny little rope around our waists." Sarah pauses, a shadow of remembered fear fallen across her features. "Well. Backing off a mountain doesn't come naturally. It takes a lot of moral support and trust in one's companions to get a person to do that."

Sarah's drop into midair was followed by what she recalls as "a tense afternoon." First of all, a couple of her fellow adventurers took the cliff leap and found themselves suspended vertiginously between rock and sky, unable to scramble up or down. "Then after those guys got stranded in the rappel and our hearts were in our throats, it started hailing, and then lightning. I said, well, I am not going on the river in lightning. And the guys in my group said, Look, it's mostly hitting the top of the canyon. Way above us." Sarah stops, shakes her head, and recounts in a low drawl, "So I said, 'When you're talking about lightning and water, *mostly* just is not *good* enough.'

"But we all got in the rafts anyway and paddled, and I was so cold and so tired and so *numb,* I didn't care whether we ever got to camp or not." Camp was yet another opportunity to sleep out solo, under the trees in the freezing wet. "I think that day was about as low as morale ever got," Sarah says. One of her cohorts on that trip, the world-record-holding hot-air balloonist Maxie Anderson, was "lovely and cheerful and *utterly* fearless." Two years later, Anderson died when an electrical storm felled his balloon in northern France, near the end of a transatlantic race.

Surviving her vacations gives Sarah a tremendous high. "Once you've done it—jumped backward over the side of a mountain, slept out on the ground in storms for a few nights, gotten through the white water and the rope courses and the rock climbing and all the rest of it . . . well, the euphoria is really something. It's exhilarating because you've done things you never thought you could do. And you and your companions become a very close-knit group, because you have had to depend on each other in some very tough spots. It gives the whole bunch of you a bond that's separate from work, outside of work. And on Wall Street that is all too rare."

AS OFTEN AS NOT, women who are inclined to cultivate one outside interest tend, over time, to add others to the list. When she's not working, or jumping backward over cliffs, Sarah builds and furnishes intricate dollhouses for her daughters. Money manager Lilia Clemente raises orchids at her home in suburban New Jersey. She also collects Korean art, and writes poetry—although so far not for publication.

Apparently on the theory that one good turn demands another, some female Wall Streeters turn up on the boards of directors of myriad not-for-profit corporations. Take Davia Temin. An erstwhile Dukakis Finance Committee co-chairman, Davia also sits on the boards of half a dozen organizations that include the Sartorius Dance Company in New York City and, in Washington, D.C., the Overseas Education Fund. The latter is a grant-giving entity that helps women in Third World countries to start and develop their own businesses.

That kind of community spirit holds out certain advantages that go beyond the warm glow of helping one's fellows. Ellen Lee, the Ernst & Co. investment banker, has served as a director of the East Orange General Hospital Foundation, in East Orange, New Jersey, since 1981. She's also a trustee and chairman of the academic affairs committee of Caldwell College. They're obligations that eat up a fair portion of her free time, but, for women who aspire to join corporate boards of directors, Ellen recommends nonprofit boards as a kind of apprenticeship: "People who have served on boards of big hospitals and universities have had to grapple with very big issues, and big problems. It's invaluable experience. And, once you've done a good job on a nonprofit board, people do assume you'll be equally professional in a corporate boardroom."

Belonging to nonprofit boards is also a way to meet movers and shakers. Ellen's fellow trustees at Caldwell, for instance, have included a managing director of Morgan Stanley, a partner in Peat Marwick Mitchell, a former vice chairman of Schering-Plough, the chairman of Midlantic Bank, and the chairman of Henderson Industries. "These are not bad contacts," observes Ellen. "It's natural for someone who needs an investment banker to say, hm, well, I know Ellen. . . . But I certainly wouldn't suggest joining a nonprofit board exclusively to enhance your business. You have to be dedicated to it. And it can be tremendously satisfying."

Because they frequently harbor an affinity for the arts that dates back to their college days—when many thought they'd pursue some sort of "women's work"—women seem particularly drawn to helping out nonprofit groups that offer aid and encouragement to nascent artists. And, as Wall Streeters, they bring to the table precisely the financial acumen and administrative competence that artists often notoriously lack. Barbara Shattuck, when she isn't doing deals or stumping for the Democratic party, puts in as many *pro bono* hours as she can at the Parrish Art Museum, near her summer house in the Hamptons. In 1982, she helped to found a nonprofit group called the Seltzer Foundation, whose purpose was to grant money to as-yet-undiscovered composers. One of the foundation's protégés, Mikel Rouse, composed and produced an album of avant-garde minimalist music that was voted one of the ten best new records of the year by the *New York Times* in 1985.

One surefire way to broaden one's horizons is to get away from Wall Street's daily hustle altogether for a while. In March of 1988, Carol Einiger began a one-year leave of absence from First Boston to become a visiting professor and executive-in-residence at Columbia Business School. She taught a course she had designed, called "Contemporary Dilemmas in Investment Banking," to twenty graduate students. Carol had every intention of going back to Wall Street, but, as she put it, "I needed a sabbatical after fifteen years."

In rare instances, the search for a well-balanced life leads to a whole new career. When that happens, it's the result of long contemplation and planning. Leslie Christian, the erstwhile English teacher who started up Salomon Brothers' futures department in 1979, left the firm in 1988 to go back to her native Washington State and study for a master's degree in art history. She is keenly fond of Chinese art, and hoped eventually to run an art gallery that would deal in it. The move came as a shock to Leslie's co-workers, but her friends could see it coming, gradually, from a long way off.

One clue was Leslie's apartment in New York, a two-story loft in the part of Manhattan known as the Flatiron District. It's a funky neighborhood just north of Greenwich Village, chockablock with art-supply stores, bookshops, and photography labs—not yet invaded by racquetball-playing young professionals. Leslie's neighbors included a distinguished violinist and the painter Julian Schnabel. Her place, at an immeasurable psychic remove from the electronic hurly-burly of the trading floor, could easily have belonged to a successful poet, or a working musician. High-ceilinged, quiet, it was a calming space, sparingly furnished, almost ascetic.

On a winter evening during the height of the bull market on Wall Street, Leslie spoke meditatively about the past, and its connection to the present. "My father wanted me to major in business in college. But I majored in English and wrote a lot of poetry. I wouldn't even *speak* to anybody from the business school. Sometimes I think that spending my college years that way put me four years behind my peers on Wall Street. But I like the person it made me. I still don't believe anybody should do any job just because it pays a lot. If that's all you get out of it, it's not worth it. You have to enjoy your life, what you do day to day."

With that in mind, once Salomon's futures operation was up and running, Leslie took a hard look at her nonstop twelve-hour workdays and decided to make a few changes in her life. "I was getting too one-dimensional," she says now. "I needed some new interests besides my career. I was getting *boring.*"

She still worked about as long and hard as she had before, and her higher-ups evidently noticed no slacking-off: in January of 1987 she was named one of six directors at Salomon Brothers, a title that is just one notch below the top tier, managing directors. But Leslie also succeeded in fitting in a few other things—travel, for one. She started to take more skiing trips, and visited more friends in other cities. She also went on her first-ever Caribbean vacation, to a private island near Tortola. A few months later, she traveled in China for two weeks with a pair of friends. In preparation for that trip, Leslie worked at learning to speak Mandarin, studying with a Chinese tutor one night a week.

But her main love, financial futures aside, was music. In common with countless other American children, Leslie took years of piano lessons, quitting when she reached high school. As part of her campaign against one-dimensionality, she started taking lessons again. A darkly shining grand piano stood on a carnelian-red Persian rug at one end of her living room. "I have always loved music. It's been easier to take it up again than I thought it would be—mostly because I'm more motivated and disciplined about practicing now than when I was a kid. It's something I really *want* to do, now." She practices mostly on weekends: "I plan to be home a lot of weeknights, but I'm usually not." She plays classical music, particularly Bach. "My second favorite kind of music to listen to"—she admits this a little sheepishly—"is country-and-western. Jimmy Buffett. The Amazing Rhythm Aces, who aren't even together as a band anymore. And the wonderful women country singers, Reba McIntire, Crystal Gayle. Those lonely ladies."

Leslie's fondness for music soon took an administrative turn. She was named president of the Concert Artists Guild, after serving as a volunteer on the board of directors for a couple of years. A nonprofit group that sponsors promising classical musicians, the Guild is a high-powered part of the New York music establishment. Such luminaries as Leonard Bernstein, Van Cliburn, Neville Marriner, and Jessye Norman sit on its advisory board, and Guild doings are keenly vetted by conductors and opera-company directors around the country and in Europe, who are eager to spot new talent. Every April, the Guild holds an international competition. The winners are usually young, brilliant, and hungry, and they receive prizes that include a lump sum of cash, the free services of a booking agency for a full year, and—perhaps best of all—a lavishly produced concert under Guild auspices.

Those concerts were staged, until recently, at Carnegie Recital Hall, moving in 1987 to Merkin Hall, a small, acoustically remarkable theater near Lincoln Center for the Performing Arts. "The electricity in the air at these things is just fantastic," Leslie said at the time. She loved the close hum of a dark hall where an intriguing mix of dim faces—students, suburbanites, socialites—settle down breathless for the first sweet sound from the lone figure in the only pool of light. "Everyone in the audience knows they're hearing the beginning of something exciting. The young artist on the stage could be the next Evelyn Lear." Lear, the great soprano, launched her operatic career by winning the Guild competition thirty-six years ago.

Although the annual contest and the ensuing concerts are the centerpiece of the Guild's activity, the organization helps out young musicians in other ways too. A rapidly growing program, one that was particularly dear to Leslie, offers career-development workshops that acquaint budding concert artists with the nitty-gritty business of making a living, steering them toward paying jobs and patrons with deep pockets. Notes Ellen Highstein, the Guild's executive director, "Classical music is an intensely competitive field, because there are just so many more musicians than there are jobs. Most often, people come out of music schools and conservatories with lots of skill and talent, but without the faintest idea of how to turn that into a career."

The talks Leslie gave at Guild workshops, Highstein explains, were aimed at getting the assembled company of artists, dedicated but unworldly as they are, to think about, well, *selling* themselves. One point Leslie always made is that, in every town in America, there are bound to be at least a few wealthy people, or a civic-minded corporation, who would take pleasure in sponsoring a gifted local musician if the idea was presented to them in the right way. At one workshop in Oberlin, Ohio, Highstein recalls that a skeptic in the audience objected, "But I don't *know* any rich people." "Well," Leslie replied, "you know me, don't you?" Following up on that exchange, and others like it, Leslie held small recitals—she called them "musicales"—in her own apartment, and introduced her protégés to select groups of well-heeled guests.

It was Leslie's involvement with the Concert Artists Guild that got her thinking about a career in the arts. While she's working in that direction, now that she's settled in Seattle, she's also doing volunteer work for the National Kidney Foundation and the Cancer Research Institute. She's still on the board of directors of the Concert Artists Guild, and still plays the piano. In June of 1989, she began putting in thirty-six hours a week helping to run New Beginnings, a shelter for battered women. Founded in 1976, New Beginnings offers medical and legal assistance, counseling, and day care for women who have fled abuse at home and are trying to start over.

Leslie's progression from futures-trading boss to art student and philanthropist may seem curious and, to a casual observer, strangely sudden. But it had its origins in a feeling many Wall Street women share, though most are unlikely ever to act on it in so radical a way. It's a powerful sense that human beings are, or ought to be, more than just the sum of their raises, promotions, and bonuses—even on Wall Street, or perhaps especially there.

Long before she thought seriously of quitting her job, Leslie put it this way: "You know, it's almost impossible to justify a career on Wall Street as socially beneficial. It's really *important* to participate in something outside yourself. Something that can help somebody else. Something beyond your own narrow personal gain.

"You hear a lot of talk on the Street about burnout. Everyone thinks people burn out because of the hours and the stress, from just not being able to handle the pressure anymore. But it seems to me that the real cause of burnout is something else. It's a profound *boredom*. An existential boredom. A sense that all you're doing every day, all you're knocking yourself out for, is generating a great big inflated income. And you have nothing else to show for it." Then she drew a deep breath and added: "When I die, I don't want my epitaph to read, 'She made a hell of a lot of money. Period.'"

Karen Robards knows that feeling well. Unlike Leslie, though, she was moved to embark on a philanthropic career by a life-altering event that might have been tragic: her son David was born, in 1983, with both a potentially fatal heart defect and Down's Syndrome. Karen was a principal in corporate finance at Morgan Stanley when David underwent open-heart surgery at the harrowingly tender age of eleven months. He survived, and went on to thrive in a special nursery school run by Columbia University for children with learning disabilities. But, when the time came to start thinking about kindergarten, Karen recalls, "We looked around for a school and realized that there was *nothing* available in Manhattan for such a child. We would have had to send him away somewhere, and we didn't want to do that."

Instead, Karen and her husband Tom took matters in hand and started their own school. Affiliated with the Roman Catholic Diocese of New York, the Cooke School for Special Education—named after the late Terence Cardinal Cooke—opened its doors in September of 1987 with $300,000 in funds that Karen had raised herself. Each day, in a bright toy-strewn classroom on West 52nd Street, her son David and thirteen other learning-disabled kids fingerpaint, play word games, and learn the alphabet, much like kindergartners everywhere else. Before Karen and Tom came along, these children would have been either institutionalized or sent to schools a long bus ride from their homes.

Karen left Morgan Stanley in July of 1987. She still has a few investment-banking clients, whose accounts she handles part time under the rubric Robards & Co. But her real career is building a bigger and better Cooke School, which takes a whole lot of fund raising. Technically part of a parochial school, the program is open to children of all faiths, and offers scholarships to those whose families couldn't ordinarily afford it. Partly because of a specially trained faculty that includes a psychologist and a speech therapist, the annual cost of the program runs to about $10,000 per child. "We have a long waiting list of children we want to bring in," says Karen, "and every time we accept a new child, we have to raise more money."

A few celebrities have pitched in, like actor Dustin Hoffman, who gave $25,000 to the cause. Nor have Karen's Wall Street connections been for nought: Morgan Stanley, Merrill Lynch, and Salomon Brothers have given cash, while Donaldson, Lufkin & Jenrette donated money and staffers' time to produce a brochure that describes the school's mission. Eventually, Karen wants to expand the Cooke School to accommodate students from ages five through eighteen. "We know these kids *can* learn," she says. "We just want them to have the chance to do it—and to live happy, independent lives. That's what it's all about."

The majority of female financiers seem likely to keep right on juggling professional ambition with personal fulfillment, and trying not to drop any of the oranges. For many, the show has already been going on for decades, and the curtain isn't anywhere near ready to fall. Consider Lilia Clemente, for one. During her stint at the Ford Foundation in the late sixties, she made an indelible mark on the way other large nonprofit organizations, including Harvard University, manage their investments. Impressed by the Ford Foundation's international savvy, portfolio managers at other big foundations say, they adopted more sophisticated research methods and a firmer grasp of the opportunities for profit abroad. Lilia has spent some of her spare time in recent years helping other nonprofit groups bone up on the world financial markets, and she would like to do much more of that. She has also begun teaching security analysts from Asia, particularly from Thailand, how to cope with the willy-nilly growth that has come in on a *tsunami* of Western capital. She hopes to expand her teaching as well. And she is an active board member of the Women's World Bank, a nonprofit institution begun in 1974 to guarantee loans to women, especially in Third World countries, who want to start their own businesses. "So far," Lilia says with obvious pride, "we have no default problem whatsoever." It's a record that many huge commercial banks, including Citicorp and Chase Manhattan, might well envy.

In common with Leslie Christian and Karen Robards, whom she has never met, Lilia has done some hard thinking about how she wants her epitaph to read; and she has reached a similar conclusion. "When I'm gone, I don't want a gravestone that says, 'Here lies Lilia. She ran these mutual funds and made lots of profits.' I'd rather have one that says, 'Here lies Lilia. She made a difference in the world.'" Then she adds, with a twinkling grin: "'And she had a lot of fun doing it.'"

M I G H T   W O R K A H O L I S M   on Wall Street become an anachronism? To be sure, the business will never return to the languid country-club pace that prevailed before the deregulation of the securities industry began in 1975. Yet, since the Crash of 1987, an unaccustomed quiet has reigned in lots of trading rooms and offices. That means that thousands of hard-driving male Wall Streeters are finally getting a chance to look up from their computer screens and spreadsheets, and to suspect that all work—with no countervailing outside passions—makes Jack a dull banker, and perhaps a rather unhappy one as well.

In this connection, the layoffs that followed—or, at Salomon

Brothers, preceded—the Crash of 1987 seem to have had a psycho-logical impact far exceeding their actual numbers. "It's true some deadwood was let go," notes a female investment banker at Solly. "But a lot of very good, talented people lost their jobs, too. So every-one who was spared was saying, 'Hey, I'm putting in sixteen hours a day around here and I'm *still* not safe? Nobody's safe anymore.' It sure as hell makes you think twice about what you're doing."

In 1988, then, Wall Streeters of both sexes were spotted slipping out the door at unwontedly early evening hours, intent on a child's school play, or a spouse's graduation from night school, or even—yes!—a dinner date.

Nor was that the most startling development. Late in the year, Eric Gleacher, Morgan Stanley's mergers-and-acquisitions boss, took the singular step of encouraging all young M.B.A.s in his employ to join up with Outward Bound, the same nonprofit organization that leads Sarah Boehmler on her wilderness treks. In New York, Outward Bound began a program that teamed budding financiers and inner-city teenagers for three-day educa-tional adventures. These included rowing a lifeboat on the East River, running a marathon around the reservoir in Central Park, and spending a night in sleeping bags at an Army base in deepest Brooklyn.

The ostensible point of all this was to teach leadership and teamwork to the kids, and the Morgan Stanley contingent doubt-less gleaned a few new skills as well. But the real agenda was to demonstrate that the best investment bankers, in Eric Gleacher's memorable words, "are not nerds or weenies who work seven days a week." Who'd have thought it?

Goldman, Sachs's top management, too, has taken steps to accom-modate employees' personal concerns—including, notably, children. Evidently mindful of the Hay Group study that predicted that only 15 percent of all new workers in the year 2000 would be white males, Goldman began planning in 1988 to offer day care to employees with kids—a move other Wall Street houses had as yet barely contemplated—and has shown no signs of stopping there.

Perhaps there is no zealot like a convert. Goldman's human-resources chief Doris Smith notes: "Men really are not used to looking at the big picture. Now they're realizing that in the years ahead they could lose at least 50 percent of the available talent out there if they don't change their old ways of thinking. And, if they want that talent, they have to evaluate what it is going to cost them. It's just like any other business decision."

Complicating matters is the fact that women are no longer the only businesspeople whose career decisions are influenced by the pull of family life. In corporate America as a whole, the late eighties saw many male members of the baby-boom generation confronting the same hard choices—partly because their wives, with demanding, well-paid jobs of their own, began expecting a lot more cooperation on the home front than previous generations of executive men had ever been asked to provide. "To gain warrior status at work, men are supposed to put in sixty or seventy hours a week," noted Robert Kelley, a business-school professor at Carnegie-Mellon University. "But they're also supposed to be equal partners with their wives, committed to their kids and in touch with their feelings." As the highest ranks of corporations gradually fill up with beleaguered boomers, Kelley predicted, a new set of values would prevail: "In the future, the very best managers will be those who keep their work lives under control, while the ones who brag about how much time they spend at the office will be viewed as disorganized."

That unaccustomed ethos may be slower to take hold on Wall Street than elsewhere. Yet, even before the stock market's fall from glory, certain muted rumblings suggested that some financiers were growing restless. In mid-June of 1987, when Wall Street was still considered by many to be the only game in town, the *Wall Street Journal* printed the results of a survey of the Harvard Business School graduating class of 1969. The study's goal was to discover whether financiers well advanced in their careers, all but fourteen of whom were male, would do it all over again if offered the chance. The answer: a clear, if somewhat equivocal, "no." Many of the men said that the rewards of a life on Wall Street—the money, the perks, the prestige—were simply not worth the personal sacrifices they had made. These included persistent stress-related illnesses, and more than a few failed marriages.

Many young women, new to the Street in the eighties, took those veterans' regrets to heart. For them, though, such tales of rue carried a particular resonance. "We were the first generation of women who were told, 'Go for it! You can have it all!'—high-powered career, happy family, stimulating outside interests. There were supposed to be no limits on what we could do if we tried," says one woman who left a major investment bank in her late twenties to open a bookstore instead. "Well, guess what. Sometimes you just *can't* 'have it all.' Corporate-finance clients deserve 100 percent of your attention. So do your own children. Something's got to give."

At the same time, surveys of Harvard's 1987 crop of M.B.A.s found that they claimed to be as eager as ever to hit the Street. Yet executives at some top investment banks were already hearing a different story. Until her departure in 1987, Karen Robards chatted with hundreds of new M.B.A.s as part of Morgan Stanley's recruiting process over a period of several years. She began to notice in 1986 that *male* job candidates were asking more questions about the Wall Street lifestyle—the grueling hours, the unpredictable travel schedules, the high-stakes pressure. "They had heard how rough it was getting, and they were clearly wondering, 'Do I really want to live this way?' I was a little bit surprised," recalls Karen. "Suddenly a lot more very talented, very high-qualified young men seemed to be having their doubts about the whole thing."

By mid-1988, those doubts had become endemic. The University of Pittsburgh surveyed the June graduates of top-flight business schools, among them Harvard, Wharton, Stanford, and Chicago, to find out about their hopes for the future. The M.B.A.s were asked to rank, in order of importance, nine goals for their lives. The results were evidence of a whopping shift in yuppie values. Family, health, and ethics topped the list, with wealth way down in the number-seven slot and power in last place, an anemic number nine.

Reflecting that order of priorities, only 9 percent of the survey respondents aspired to investment-banking careers. By contrast, 19 percent wanted to go into—hold on to your hat—industrial-manufacturing management. For women, that trend holds more than a little irony. High-ranking female executives are even scarcer in manufacturing than in finance, so steering clear of Wall Street will hardly guarantee women M.B.A.s a smoother road ahead. Many will no doubt decide to start companies of their own. Between 1980 and 1986, according to an Internal Revenue Service study released in late 1988, the number of businesses in the United States owned by women grew from 2.5 million to 4.1 million, a 64 percent increase. Those companies' total sales doubled over the same period from $36 billion to $72 billion. "Women-owned businesses are currently the fastest-growing segment of the economy," said James Abdnor, who was then the head of the U.S. Small Business Administration in Washington. "And what we are seeing in these IRS figures is just the beginning." Tellingly, Abdnor was succeeded in May of 1989 by Susan Engeleiter, a former Wisconsin state legislator and the SBA's first female chief.

In the post-Crash era on Wall Street, wealth and power remain quite popular, thank you. And, in a business that is made of money, they no doubt always will be. But they are no longer all there is.

Observes Barbara Shattuck: "Now that so many people have been laid off, or realize they could be laid off, from jobs they have worked so hard at—and now that a lot of people are going to be doing less business and making less money—well, I have seen a lot of reevaluating going on. People are saying, 'Who am I?' You can't define yourself by your job so easily anymore."

Most women never did. If introspection and the search for a well-balanced life are indeed the trend of the nineties, then Wall Street women will be well ahead of the pack. With their habitual concern for matters other than monetary, they may yet come to be regarded by their male colleagues not as a strange and unworthy minority but as the harbingers of a new and more rational order.

INDEX

A Note About the Author

Anne B. Fisher is an award-winning business journalist and a former associate editor of Fortune *magazine. Her work has also appeared in* Inc., Savvy, Ms., Barron's, *and* The New York Times Book Review. *She lives in New York City.*

A Note on the Type

This book was set in a typeface called Baskerville. The face is
a contemporary interpretation of types cast from molds made for
John Baskerville (1706–1775) from his designs. Baskerville's
original face was one of the forerunners of the type style known to
printers as "modern face"—a "modern" of the period A.D. 1800.

Composed by Superior Type,
Champaign, Illinois

Printed and bound by Fairfield Graphics,
Fairfield, Pennsylvania

Designed by Valarie J. Astor